A Life in Classrooms

A Life in Classrooms

PHILIP W. JACKSON
AND THE PRACTICE OF EDUCATION

EDITED BY

David T. Hansen
Mary Erina Driscoll
René V. Arcilla

TEACHERS COLLEGE PRESS

Teachers College, Columbia University
New York and London

Published by Teachers College Press, 1234 Amsterdam Avenue, New York, NY 10027

Library of Congress Cataloging-in-Publication Data

A life in classrooms : Philip W. Jackson and the practice of education / edited by David T. Hansen, Mary Erina Driscoll, René V. Arcilla.
   p. cm.
  Papers from a conference in honor of Philip W. Jackson entitled Images of Teaching in the 21st Century, held in New York City on October 24 and 25, 2003.
  Includes bibliographical references and index.
  ISBN-13: 978-0-8077-4776-6 (pbk : alk. paper)
  ISBN-13: 978-0-8077-4777-3 (cloth : alk. paper)
  1. Teaching. 2. Teachers—United States. 3. Jackson, Philip W. (Philip Wesley), 1928- I. Hansen, David T. II. Driscoll, Mary Erina, 1956- III. Arcilla, René Vincente, 1956- IV. Jackson, Philip W. (Philip Wesley), 1928- V. Title.

LB1025.3.L548 2007
371.1—dc22   2007001061

ISBN 978-0-8077-4776-6 (paper)
ISBN 978-0-8077-4777-3 (cloth)

Printed on acid-free paper
Manufactured in the United States of America

14 13 12 11 10 09 08 07   8 7 6 5 4 3 2 1

Contents

Acknowledgments

THIS BOOK is the outcome of a conference in honor of Philip W. Jackson entitled "Images of Teaching in the 21st Century." The conference convened in New York City on October 24 and 25, 2003. It featured presentations by an array of scholars, some of them former students of Professor Jackson, from many fields in education. They have converted their presentations into the essays that now appear in this volume.

The editors would like to thank the presenters and participants at what all agree was a remarkable occasion befitting the career of an exemplary scholar, teacher, and person. We thank the Steinhardt School of Education, New York University, and Teachers College, Columbia University, for their support of the conference, and we are particularly grateful to Dean Mary Brabeck of the Steinhardt School and to Dean Darlyne Bailey of Teachers College. We thank Brian Ellerbeck and his colleagues at Teachers College Press for their excellent editorial and production work. Thanks also to Tanzina Taher, secretary for the Program in Philosophy and Education, Teachers College, for her able assistance with the preparation of the manuscript. The publication of the book has been made possible by a grant from the Spencer Foundation (the contributors to the volume remain fully responsible for its contents). All royalties earned by the book will be contributed to the John Dewey Society.

To Watch the Water Clear

Mary Erina Driscoll, David T. Hansen, and René V. Arcilla

THIS BOOK is a labor of many hands, hearts, and minds. It is a book in honor of a scholar, a teacher, a person who has left an indelible mark on several generations of educational researchers and practitioners.

At one level, the book is the product of a 2-day conference in honor of this individual: Philip W. Jackson. On another and much larger level , this book has been developing for years, the fruit not of a 2-day conference but rather of a lifetime that has produced a vivid conversation—and, in the form of the book, a bountiful rejoinder to the ever-evolving scholarship of Philip W. Jackson. On the autumn morning we gathered in New York, the mood was neither elegiac nor hortatory, but rather one that marveled at the continuous connections across many generations of scholars influenced by Jackson's work. It is this latter spirit we seek to capture in our book. Thus, we also include several chapters by some of Jackson's other colleagues and students. We offer readers from across today's educational communities an invitation to discover for the first time, or to engage again, the power and significance in Jackson's career accomplishments.

TO WATCH THE WATER CLEAR

We begin with a line by Robert Frost. His poem "The Pasture" dates from his second published collection of poetry, entitled *North of Boston* (published 1915). Widely anthologized, the first of the poem's two stanzas read:

I'm going out to clean the pasture spring;
I'll only stop to rake the leaves away
(and wait to watch the water clear, I may):
I shan't be gone long.—You come too.

Why poetry to herald a collection in honor of Jackson? And why this poem in particular? We chose this epigraph for three reasons, each of which captures, we believe, a key aspect of Jackson's scholarship.

First, poetry is for Jackson one of the essential ways of knowing the world. This point is particularly clear in his later work that brings together the philosophy of John Dewey and an understanding of the arts to glean new insights for the experience of education as we come to know it. Frost was an early favorite of Jackson's, as his readers will know, but our choice to draw from him from among many other distinguished poets is appropriate because both Frost and Jackson are writers who continually revisit and reconsider insights gleaned from previous stages of their careers. They frame with a richer, and wiser, lens those aspects of experience that seem all too familiar and simple, until we begin to see the layers of meaning embedded in them. Frost's words explaining his 1942 selection of a set of poems drawn from his early work seem apt for Jackson as well: "The interest, the pastime, was to learn if there had been any divinity shaping my ends and if I had been building better than I knew." The richness in the book we present to the educational community attests to the fact that from the very beginning of his scholarly life, Jackson built well.

Second, the themes in Frost's "The Pasture" map nicely onto some of the characteristics of Jackson's ways of working through intellectual problems. Like the speaker in the poem, Jackson often calls our attention to the most ordinary, even the homeliest, object in view, dating from the days when he first sat in the back of a classroom amidst the chalk dust. But the speaker is not going to just *look* at the pasture spring; rather, he will clean it, rake the leaves away, do something, engage and act upon the natural phenomenon. That impulse towards purposive activity that, once undertaken, may reveal unimagined insights marks Jackson's work as well. Attention to the ordinary permeates Jackson's work, whether it is counting the number of student questions that go unanswered in a classroom or "counting" the evolving meanings in John Dewey's four different introductions to his philosophical opus, *Experience and Nature*. The work of a scholar, in other words, may start with simple and homely facts, and acts, but if one is prepared to wait and to attend, to let time and wonder do their work, we may indeed watch the water clear to reveal something fundamental. *What* is seen becomes the subject of several of the essays that follow in this volume, which variously attest to both the light cast by Jackson's vision and the ever-present darkness it (like every vision) can only partially illuminate.

Third, the poem ends as a form of invitation: "You come too." More than anything else, we believe that Jackson's work has been an invitation to other scholars and teachers to look anew and to look carefully at familiar realities of education and of experience. It is our collective fortune, as an educational community, that so many who have known Jackson as scholar and as teacher have taken up that invitation. This book, then, celebrates not merely the accomplishment but also the generativity of Jackson's work. It captures the long reach of his influence throughout the community of scholars and practitioners in education and related fields.

THE COURSE OF A LIFE

It may be that Jackson's affinity for poetry grew out his early experience with music. His scholarly biography might gloss over his experience as a child vaudevillian and a college band singer, but one could argue that in reading his work, something in that early development attuned his ear early and well to the rhythms of language. Likewise, Jackson's brief career as a teacher after graduating from a state teacher's college in New Jersey left him permanently imprinted with the sensibilities of classroom life and perpetually curious about those who live there. The more standard elements of his vita emerge in bits and pieces throughout the chapters in the book, with far richer detail than a chronological recitation can convey. Thus, in the pages that follow the reader will find embedded references to Jackson's early career as a psychologist, first as a student at Teachers College, Columbia University, and later as a young professor at the University of Chicago (following a year at Wayne Sate University). Here, too, readers will see the maturing academic who helped craft a new scholarship of education, built on his disciplinary roots but uniquely situated in schools, and brilliantly announced in the classic *Life in Classrooms* (1968), widely acknowledged as giving an enormous impetus to what we now call qualitative research. The chapters ahead trace why Jackson's work has had a worldwide impact (*Life in Classrooms* has been translated into a number of European and Asian languages). The chapters also touch on other well-known works Jackson produced: *The Practice of Teaching* (1986), a highly original set of essays on teaching, including the now-classic discussion of "the mimetic and the transformative" in educating; *Untaught Lessons* (1992b), based on the Sachs Lectures at Teachers College and featuring a close look at the experience of teaching and learning as captured in both empirical research and humanistic inquiry; *John Dewey and the Lessons of Art* (1998b), an instantaneous hit in fields such as art education, aesthetics, and Dewey scholarship; and *John Dewey and the Philosopher's Task* (2002b), based on his John Dewey Society Lecture, and a trenchant, fine-grained study of Dewey's conception of philosophy as a critical practice of life. Jackson is also co-author of other highly influential works, such as *Creativity and Intelligence* (Getzels & Jackson, 1962) and *The Moral Life of Schools* (Jackson, Boostrom, & Hansen, 1993), whose contours readers can also trace in the chapters ahead.

Readers also catch telling glimpses of Jackson in other roles, including as director of the University of Chicago Laboratory School and as dean of the School of Education at that same university. One must read between the lines to see some of his other remarkable accomplishments: president of the American Educational Research Association, member of the National Academy of Education, president of the John Dewey Society, and more. What comes through clearly throughout is Jackson's critical role as a teacher to generations of scholars, not merely through his work as a professor for over 40 years at the University of Chicago, but also through his ability to develop new ways of seeing that opened the eyes of so many educators.

THE CHAPTERS

The authors of the chapters that lie ahead address Jackson's influence on their perception: literally, how they came to *see* the world of educational practice, or how they came to *see* what is entailed in the act of research. The authors document Jackson's influence not just on their own work but also on the larger field of educational research and practice. They address these contributions and specify implications for further work that can continue to deepen the critical tradition Jackson so powerfully helped to initiate.

A second theme heard throughout these chapters concerns what comes to be *known* or *understood* "as the water clears." The authors ask: What happens once the invitation to inquiry has been accepted—namely, to pay attention to the everyday rather than solely to the dramatic—and the work of scholarship launched? The authors make plain how Jackson has influenced our ways of knowing in education as much as he has our ways of seeing. Several authors portray how Jackson's vision of education and of inquiry helped them to see a familiar subject in an entirely new and more promising light. Others illuminate how Jackson's approach to understanding and knowing finds expression in the distinctive ways he wrote about curriculum or about the work of other scholars, especially John Dewey.

In Chapters 1–3, Lee Shulman, Linda Darling-Hammond, and David Hansen address Jackson's influence on their ways of seeing as inquirers. They show how Jackson helped them reconsider fundamental questions about the purposes of education. They illuminate how influential a great scholar's work can be on others who seek to practice the arts of research. Maxine Greene and Robert Boostrom, in Chapters 4 and 5, respectively, examine Jackson's impact on how we perceive imagination and thinking in education. Greene highlights Jackson's highly imaginative work, fusing her commentary with a reflection on the values in critical imagination for our time. Boostrom portrays Jackson's many ways of thinking about education, in so doing shedding light on the nature of thinking itself.

In Chapters 6–8, René Arcilla, Thomas James, and Mary Erina Driscoll address Jackson's impact on how we think about several key educational tasks and roles. Arcilla takes us inside Jackson's university classroom to paint him at work as a teacher of enduring influence. James reveals Jackson's impact on research on schools by describing his own experience as a schoolboy in the very institution where Jackson was serving as director of the school. Driscoll examines Jackson's writings about schools to glean lessons about educational leadership that cast new light on this crucial dimension of practice. In Chapters 9–11, Lauren Sosniak, Karen Zumwalt, and David Granger and Craig Cunningham shed light on Jackson's enduring influence on several key fields of educational research. Sosniak and Zumwalt attend in distinctive ways to Jackson's pioneering scholarship on curriculum. Granger and Cunningham illuminate Jackson's important work on John Dewey.

The epilogue to the book constitutes a personal reminiscence by a friend and long-term conversational partner of Jackson, Elliot Eisner. The chapter fittingly brings the book to a close by reminding us that research and teaching are conducted by individual human beings who hope to influence, at the end of the day, other individual human beings. Eisner's chapter shows us that a key task of education is to attend to each person as fully as possible, a value that further characterizes Jackson's lifelong accomplishment.

CONCLUDING NOTE

We began with words from Frost, and we close with them. In his introductory essay to the 1939 edition of his *Collected Poems*, entitled "The Figure A Poem Makes," Frost (1939/1972) writes: "It should be of the pleasure of a poem itself to tell how it can. The figure a poem makes. It begins in delight and ends in wisdom" (p. 394).

This project began in delight as we assembled that October morning in New York. The occasion was so significant that it led to a joint collaboration by two leading schools of education in the nation. The project culminates in the chapters that follow, which we believe will help readers come to grips that much more with the meaning and necessity of wisdom in education. As Frost further writes: "The figure is the same as for love. . . . It begins in delight, it inclines to the impulse, it assumes direction with the first line laid down, it runs a course of lucky events, and ends in a clarification of life—not necessarily a great clarification, such as sects and cults are founded on, but in a momentary stay against confusion" (p. 394).

The chapters assembled here are offered as an invitation to think, to learn, and to reflect on the career of an individual whose contributions represent far more than a momentary stay against confusion. The authors have taken that journey together, always in the visible or sometimes invisible company of the scholar whose work we honor. You come too.

CHAPTER 1

The Impossible Fullness of the Empty Classroom: A Letter of Appreciation

Lee S. Shulman

IT SEEMS as though it was only yesterday that Philip Jackson was the youngest tenured member of the faculty in Judd Hall at the University of Chicago. And I suspect I was about the youngest graduate student at the time. But as my medical school colleagues later reminded me at Michigan State, youth is a "self-limiting disorder," which is the fancy medical way of saying you grow out of it.

The organization of the meeting in New York to pay tribute to Philip Jackson has moved many of us, especially because of its location in the shadow of one of America's most revered and unusual institutions: the Second Avenue Deli (which is on 10th Street and 2nd Avenue and I recommend it very highly). While I was Jackson's student, I was still working at a family delicatessen in Logan Square in Chicago, where some of my most important field work was done.

The topic of the conference in Jackson's honor is "images of teaching." But there are no images of teaching that are possible if you can't see, and this lesson was Jackson's most powerful contribution to all of us. Jackson taught us to look, to see, to find the patterns and regularities and themes in the buzzing, blooming confusion of everyday life in classrooms. He showed us how to appreciate both the triumphs and the toxicities associated with that world. And perhaps most important of all, he taught us that when one looks and sees and engages with a phenomenon in that way, one becomes obligated not only to understand it, but to care about it. And that's a theme that I will return to several times in this essay.

Let me begin first with the notion of seeing. How do you get smart about something? To help us understand that, let me turn to one of our earliest texts on method. Here is a passage from Genesis 1:1–5:

> When God began to create heaven and earth—the earth being unformed and void, with darkness over the surface of the deep and a wind from God sweeping over the water—God said, "Let there be light"; and there was light. God saw that the light was good, and God separated the light from the darkness. God called the light Day, and the darkness He called Night. And there was evening and there was morning, a first day. (JPS Hebrew–English Tanakh, 1999)

Perhaps that should've been called "On Method" instead of "Genesis." What a lovely lesson about method. And it's one that is exemplified in Jackson's work. Like many of us who have known him, for me, the "book" of Genesis, from which I am going to be drawing most of my remarks, is my original, tattered copy of *Life in Classrooms* (a book which would be easier to read if I discarded that ragged outside cover, but I just can't part with it) (Jackson, 1968).

First of all, *this* treatise on method helps us understand that before we start trying to understand something, it is formless. It is void, it is undefined. It is a positive, aggressive, assertive act that *gives* meaning, that makes it possible to see. And what makes it possible to see is light. And the light is supplied from the outside.

The second thing that Jackson taught us is that when you sit in the darkness of the classroom, the light grows only if you are prepared to remain there, to persist there. And the longer you look, the more light you see.

But there's a third message. In the midst of this description of light and darkness, there is the notion that "it was good"—that to sit and to cast light also requires that you make moral judgments, that you be concerned with issues of goodness. And when one reads *Life in Classrooms*, one is keenly aware that it is not written by a dispassionate observer. Its author is already someone quite concerned with matters of goodness.

But notice that by the second verse of Genesis, God starts making distinctions. Because to move from looking to seeing, and from seeing to understanding, is to start making distinctions and *naming* things: "light," "darkness." *Life in Classrooms* begins with a sense of the chaotic, overwhelming mys tery of the classroom and ends by beginning to offer us the names for things, ideas that organize that chaos and help us both understand and *care* for it.

It's again no accident that a bit later in Genesis, not much later, the first responsibility that God gives his new creation, Adam, is the responsibility for naming the animals. In naming things, we become *responsible* for them. To look deeply is to become responsible; to name is to become even more responsible.

In this sense, I find Jackson (and this may seem paradoxical) very Baconian, because Francis Bacon, in his *Arguments for Induction*, strongly made the point that knowledge begins by looking carefully. One gains knowledge not by coming in with preconceived models of what one is studying, but by looking persistently, carefully, and patiently. Bacon also made the distinction between "experiments of fruit" and "experiments of light"; that is, experiments directed at producing some tool or solution to an immediate problem, and experiments that shed greater light on complex phenomena and lead us to understand them better. I strongly believe that Jackson is an experimentalist in a Baconian sense in that he does experiments of light.

Jackson was my teacher. He taught one of my first classes at graduate school at the University of Chicago. And with boundless courage, after I took a course in classroom research with him, he agreed to be the adviser for my master's thesis, the unforgettable *Attitudes Toward Authority and Sociometric Status Among Fourth-Grade Children*. (The movie version, *Shane*, was much more memorable.)

What was fascinating about that master's thesis is that it was a piece of psychological research, done by a budding psychologist, under the guidance of a deeply committed psychologist. And if one wants to see the source of the methods used in my master's thesis, one should look at *Creativity and Intelligence* by Jacob Getzels and Philip Jackson (Getzels & Jackson, 1962). This book offered a set of ways of making sense of the world in which one did not sit and look directly but rather used an array of psychological tools called psychometric instruments: measures of intelligence, of creativity, of attitudes, and of values. Then one created monstrous correlation matrices and computed F values, and one got smart in some very interesting ways.

Even then, Jackson was interested in what we would call the "off-diagonal" cells, by which I mean the correlation of creativity and intelligence. Jackson and Getzels were interested in those people who were high in creativity but *not* high in intelligence and those who were high in intelligence but *not* in creativity.

In that project, Jackson was already cutting against the grain. (Something that my mother taught me in the delicatessen was also the best way to treat a brisket.) It's also been his style ever since: cut *against* the grain, take the road *not* taken. While learning to be a psychologist with Jackson, he taught me a number of very important lessons. Let me mention three immediate ones before I get to the longer-term lessons that actually did not come from the Jackson I studied with, but from the Jackson he became through his subsequent scholarship.

First, he helped me recognize that what we choose to study is not a random act. What we choose to study often has a great deal to do with either the angels or the demons that we are wrestling with at the time we make the choice. I remember well when Jackson sat me down—I was a 21-year-old graduate student—and said, "You know, Lee, I don't think it's an accident that you decided to study attitudes toward authority in fourth graders." He was right. And it was an important lesson.

The second lesson Jackson taught me, and I hope this doesn't embarrass him (I don't think it will), occurred another time when he sat me down. He said, "Never forget that you are a psychologist. You're doing work in education, but we are psychologists. That's your discipline. That's how you come to understand the world." I think it's very interesting that now, almost 45 years later, both of us would very likely be seen as "lapsed" psychologists. And yet up to the moment that each of us became an emeritus in our respective institutions, we never gave up our appointment in the psychology department. Lurking inside Jackson today, the evolved philosopher, there remains the psychologist who was educated at Teachers College, Columbia University, and who educated me at the University of Chicago.

The third lesson that Jackson taught me that I have never ever forgotten is that Philip is spelled with one *l*. My problem now is that I spell all Philips with one *l*.

Jackson also almost ruined my career when I took a course with him called "Theories of Learning." We of course read Ernest Hilgard, and to this day I won't forget when he wrote on the board at the beginning of one class the full version of the Hull-Spense equation. He put it all there and then turned to us and said: "This is supposed to explain learning. Isn't this ridiculous? Let's talk about Henry Murray." And we did.

The reason Jackson almost ruined my career is that a few years later, when I interviewed for the only job that I was invited to interview for (which was an opening in learning at Michigan State), I went there thinking that because I'd taken this course with Jackson, I understood learning. I was informed that I didn't know diddly about what the rest of the world called learning. Fortunately, I had learned a great deal through Jackson and his colleagues about what the rest of the world *would* call learning a generation later.

Jackson also convinced me to withdraw from an assistantship for Benjamin Bloom that I had already accepted. Jackson was the only one I could ask about this as he was the only one I felt I could trust regarding the matter.

I didn't know Bloom. Jackson simply said, "You will be happy you made this decision." He was absolutely, absolutely correct. Later, when Ben Bloom refused to direct my dissertation because he was convinced that research on thought and problem solving was a dead end, I went back to Jackson and he guided me to my dissertation director, Fred Lighthall.

However, these experiences did not prepare me for the shock of *Life in Classrooms*. I still remember 1968. His book was coming out. (For some of us, it was a major event.) I remember opening this book and beginning to read it, keeping in mind the psychologist with whom I had trained, going from chapter to chapter and thinking, "Mr. Jackson, what in God's name did you have in mind?" This book didn't *look* like a piece of educational research. It didn't resemble it at all; it was strange, it was weird.

One has to understand that 1968 was a pivotal year. Two books like this were published by the same publisher that year. One was your *Life in Classrooms*; the other, by Louis Smith and William Geoffrey, was called *Complexities of an Urban Classroom* (Smith & Geoffrey, 1968). Both books were *qualitative* studies of teaching. In their own way, Smith and Geoffrey were even more revolutionary because Geoffrey was the pseudonym for the teacher whose classroom was being studied and who co-authored the volume. These two wild books were nurtured by a person whose name one does not often hear anymore—the education editor of Holt, Reinhardt and Winston. His name was David Boynton. Those were the days when editors really made a difference as gatekeepers and midwives, and David Boynton had the courage and the insight to support this kind of publication.

I'm going to spend most of my time in this essay discussing *Life in Classrooms*, and I am going to discuss some excerpts from it, because I think it is embryonic of all of what Jackson was to evolve through and into thus far in his career. I think we can find the seeds of his work, *all* of his work, already in this book. It also has the seeds of where the world of research on teaching has moved and where our images of teaching have come from.

Jackson clearly recognized that there was something strange about this book. In the preface, he says, "Stylistically, the book is a mélange." *Goulash* is another word for it. "Descriptions of empirical studies are interlaced with speculative asides"—people often forget that there are a lot of statistical tables in this book—"tabular materials sometimes share the page with the most unquantifiable assertions. The expository tone is hard in some sections, soft in others. But the mixture is not without purpose. Classroom life, in my judgment, is too complex an affair to be viewed or talked about from any single perspective. Accordingly, as we try to grasp the meaning of what school is like for students and teachers we must not hesitate to use all the ways of knowing at our disposal" (p. vii).

Jackson's first lesson: Schooling, classrooms, and education are far too important to be limited by any kind of methodological orthodoxy or dogmatism. As a familiar statement (attributed to the physicist Percy Bridgeman) has it, inquiry is about doing one's damndest with one's mind, no holds barred. *Life in Classrooms* is a model of that kind of attitude. Confront the problem first and let the method follow.

There are two kinds of lessons that I want to emphasize from this book, though it's rich with many others. One has to do with the introduction of an attitude of enormous respect for the teacher as someone who makes sense of classroom life. In this case, Jackson refers us to a philosopher who had a bit of influence on his thinking, John Dewey.

I think Jackson and I have the same attitude toward John Dewey. Dewey was not an ethical scholar. He regularly engaged in acts of anticipatory plagiarism with regard to *our* work. The mere fact that someone is born earlier than you gives him absolutely no right to preempt your hard-won ideas.

Jackson (1968) writes:

> In teaching, as in every craft, there are masters from whom apprentices can and should learn. Although perfect agreement on who deserves the title may not exist, it is likely that in every school system there could be found at least a handful of teachers who would be called outstanding by almost any standard. The profession as a whole might gain from such persons, but, as Dewey observed, "the successes of such individuals tend to be born and die with them; beneficial consequences extend only to those pupils who have personal contact with such gifted teachers. . . . The only way by which we can prevent such waste in the future is by methods which enable us to make an analysis of what the gifted teacher does intuitively, so that something accruing from his work can be communicated to others." (p. 115)

Jackson's lovely elaboration of this set of ideas has guided and inspired many of us for years. One can see in passages such as those quoted thus far the seeds of what cognitive psychologists have called "expert/novice" research. The work that my colleagues and I have done on what we call the "wisdom of practice" and now in the "scholarship of teaching and learning" derives *directly* from these kinds of ideas. They derive directly from Jackson's Baconian vision, which is: Don't get some theories from learning theorists and lay them on teachers in order to understand their practice. Study their practice in its own terms. Sit, listen, *watch*. Jackson's vision of educational research is his most powerful theory. Within this vision there is an even deeper insight, because what Jackson was preaching was a kind of enlightened behaviorism. (Those of us who are psychologists know there are only two kinds of psychologists: behaviorists and enlightened behaviorists.)

Jackson also makes the following observation about what it means to learn from watching and looking at teaching:

> There is a crucial difference it would seem between what the teacher does when he is alone at his desk and what he does when his room fills up with students. . . . The distinction being made here between two aspects of the teacher's work is so fundamental and has so many implications for educational matters that it deserves some kind of official recognition in the language used to describe the teaching process. [How important naming is!] The terms "interactive" and "preactive" might serve this purpose. What the teacher does vis-à-vis students could be called "interactive teaching" and what he does at other times—in an empty classroom, so to speak—could be called "preactive teaching." These terms help us keep in mind a qualitative difference that is often overlooked. (pp. 151-152)

I called Jackson some weeks before the conference in his honor because I couldn't find this quote in *Life in Classrooms* and yet I knew it was there. I ended up finding it through the help of a student of mine who couldn't have done his dissertation had Jackson not made that distinction. About 5 years after Jackson made that distinction, I told a young doctoral student at Michigan State named Robert Yinger that he could spend an entire year in one teacher's classroom trying to understand her planning. And Yinger did a memorable dissertation, in which he drew on the literature of architecture and urban planning and automobile design as he tried to understand a year's worth of interactions and observations of this teacher's efforts. Like Jackson, Yinger became a dean. He did good work before that, work that paralleled an entire generation of research on teacher planning, teacher thinking, teacher knowledge, and teacher reflection. And the roots of this body of work are in *Life in Classrooms*. And its model is the work of Philip Jackson.

The world that Jackson describes is a world that in some ways is quite frightening. It's filled with terror for both teachers and kids. At one point, Jackson asks: How do we help kids deal with this world? What can teachers do with the anonymity, the isolation, and the toxicity (Jackson's words) of classroom life?

Jackson suggests three attitudes for the teacher. First, look so carefully that you truly come to know and understand your students as individual human beings. That can help reduce the toxicity. Second, not only *know* them, but *care* about them. Third, become in your own work a model of fallibility. These are lovely admonitions not only for the teacher, but for the scholar.

Jackson's book is filled with distinctions, it's filled with namings, and it's filled with wisdom. There's an interesting irony about its standing as a piece of research on teaching. In the mid-1980s, I was preparing the opening chapter of the third handbook of research on teaching. One of the books I looked at carefully was *The Study of Teaching* (Dunkin & Biddle, 1974), which at the time (1974) was the first comprehensive account that organized the empirical research on teaching. After an opening chapter that laid

l framework, it began to systematically look at studies of
generalize, accumulate, and aggregate their findings in
ations. The work that was going to be analyzed and used for
generalizations had to meet certain scientific standards of educational
scholarship.

Here's the lovely irony. I looked at Chapters 2 through whatever of this book to see how they were using Jackson's studies of teaching and made this discovery: Jackson's work didn't meet the "standard" of research. Duncan and Biddle didn't use a single study of Jackson's as the basis for their generalizations about teaching. On the other hand, the first chapter of the book, which lays out the conceptual framework for thinking about and making sense of teaching, refers to no one more frequently than Philip Jackson!

Jackson taught us to see. Jackson taught us to look.

Bacon said he much preferred installments of light to experiments of fruit. It'd be nice if we could do both, of course. But Jackson gave us the light with which to look at teaching. (And if Mick Duncan and Bruce Biddle couldn't figure out a way to treat Jackson's findings seriously in the rest of the book, so much the worse for Mickey and for Bruce.)

There is a sense in which the proper epigraph for *Life in Classrooms* was not written until almost 25 years later. It helps us understand *why* it's so important to look. Only now can we recognize how the ethnographic turn that Jackson pioneered was such an important move in the history of research on teaching. Thanks to Jackson, we have profoundly expanded our ability to develop images of teaching.

The epigraph comes from the final section of *The Moral Life of Schools* (Jackson, Boostrom, & Hansen, 1993). In it, Jackson and his distinguished colleagues-cum-students or students-cum-colleagues make the observation that what confronts any observer of classrooms (and all of us who have observed classrooms have experienced this) is the tension between getting more and more deeply drawn in, engaged, seduced by the impassioned events going on in that setting—and somehow remaining detached enough to be a scholar. Detached enough to make sense and not (as the anthropologists talk about it) "go native," that is, be so drawn in that you can't see what you're experiencing. Jackson and his co-authors say, "This detachment must not be confused with indifference. On the contrary, it expresses a degree of caring uncommon in its intensity" (pp. 271–272).

Detachment and intense caring. What a beautifully Deweyan image and tension. One thing that accounts for its uncommonness is the time it takes in its enactment. "As we hope the contents of this book have by now amply demonstrated"—and they do—"there is no way of looking carefully at anything that goes on in schools, or anywhere else for that matter, without spending a considerable amount of time doing so" (p. 272). Jackson and his co-authors elaborate the point as follows, suggesting this posture is far removed from "idle curiosity":

> The longer we look and the more we reflect upon what we have seen . . . , the more we come to care about whatever we were looking at and reflecting upon. Thus, the act of looking and listening carefully, together with subsequent periods of reflection, not only expresses to onlookers an attitude of interest on the part of the observer; it also serves to increase the observer's genuine interest in what he or she is observing. (p. 272)

"What this means for teachers and others who work in classrooms," they go on to say, "is that the time spent in stepping aside from their roles as immediate caregivers and in trying to view their students and their classrooms from a somewhat more detached point of view is actually time invested in *adding* to their own sense of involvement in what they are doing" (p. 272; emphasis in original).

In these words we discover a profound observation about both research and about teaching: There is a balance between investment and attachment, between engaging with the classroom world deeply, intimately, and passionately, and yet stepping back and reflecting on it. That is not only the special privilege of the scholar, but it is also an image of teaching. It is an image of a professional who can both be committed and separated, who can care deeply and yet also try to understand what is going on.

I think this is the lesson of Jackson's work: The teacher's first responsibility is to know. To know his or her students. To know deeply those things that she is responsible for teaching her students. To be a learner, a scholar, an intellectual, while at the same time to be a deeply caring and committed caregiver to students. Knowledge without caring is not teaching. But caring without knowledge isn't teaching either. Anyone who tries sincerely to combine these two, the knowledge *and* the caring, and steps back to examine their own experience, will necessarily develop feelings of fallibility. It is this fallibility that we must make public and model for others because it is fallibility that makes us essentially human.

I thank Jackson for these gifts. I thank him for serving, in many ways, as a kind of methodological and substantive bridge for me to many domains of scholarship and teaching. And he and his pioneering work have been a bridge between the work of my colleague Elliot Eisner and my colleague Linda Darling-Hammond: a bridge between the goal of finding a way to enlighten the eye and finding a way to enlighten policy. It has formed a bridge between experiments of light and experiments of fruit. Jackson has given us artful tools for developing images of teaching, and for that we are all very, very grateful.

Images of Teaching: Cultivating a Moral Profession

Linda Darling-Hammond

IN THIS essay, I want to speak from the perspective of a teacher as well as a researcher and from the perspective of a student of Philip Jackson's, although I have experienced his work once or twice removed from having had the opportunity to study directly with him. Jackson has, in many ways, given me words for what I know to be true of teaching and has caused me to think more intensely about what the truth of teaching means for the practice and policy of education and for the preparation of teachers. I want to describe how Phil has given me, as Lee Shulman (Chapter 1, this volume) put it, the *words* I knew to be true of teaching from my own experience in the classroom. I also want to describe three images of teaching derived from Phil's work that have informed my work as a teacher, a researcher, a policy analyst, and a teacher educator—and that I believe should inform the efforts of others who seek to shape the educational system as well as the classroom.

The three images are: teaching as the skillful "chasing of butterflies," teaching as the cultivation of learning from and through experience—an agricultural image, and teaching as reflection on the consequences of one's actions for students—an image of contemplation leading to moral action. These images derive from an understanding of learning as grounded in experience and an understanding of teaching as a complex, reciprocal process of connecting students' many experiences with the goals of curriculum. These ways of understanding teaching and learning suggest that teachers must be keen observers of their students, sensitive to what students bring to and encounter in the classroom, and creators of curriculum that forges connections between students and the subject matter.

Furthermore, these images stand in contrast to technicist assumptions that teaching is the application of a set stimulus to evoke a standardized response and to the implications drawn by some researchers and many policymakers that teaching can be tightly prescribed—assumptions that undergird many misunderstandings of learning and teaching and often provoke dysfunctional educational policies. The images of teaching Philip Jackson has rendered so vividly suggest approaches to the organization of teaching and the preparation of teachers that should aim to develop reflective practitioners who work on behalf of their students rather than bureaucratic functionaries who are trained to follow procedures on behalf of their superiors.

TEACHING AND CHASING BUTTERFLIES

I first read Philip Jackson's work through the eyes of a teacher just beginning to become a researcher about teaching. I had taught urban middle and high school students before I completed a doctorate and began to conduct research. Reading *Life in Classrooms* provided a way for me to think more intensely about what I had experienced and to begin to transform those experiences into a perspective about how to study teaching and the work of schools. It also helped me to help others begin to understand teaching in more productive ways.

I was excited when I first read *Life in Classrooms*. It described what I had felt but what had not been affirmed in the conceptualization of teaching offered when I was learning to teach. I had been through a teacher education program in the 1970s that was based in part on "competency-based teacher education." CBTE, as it was called, tried to take the act of teaching and divide it up into dozens of little dollops of skills that one was to learn independently and practice in microteaching sessions. Some of what I learned in this program was productive and useful for me in particular ways, but, overall, it didn't really capture what I experienced in the classroom. When I read Jackson's words I nearly shouted, "Yes! This is what teaching is." The book gave me an image of teaching that resonated with what I knew, and it guided my later work. Jackson (1968) wrote:

> Teaching is an opportunistic process. Neither the teacher nor the students can predict with any certainty exactly what will happen next. Plans are forever going

> awry and unexpected opportunities for the attainment of educational goals are
> constantly emerging. . . . Although most teachers make plans in advance, they
> are aware as they make them of the likelihood of change. . . . They know, or
> come to know, that the path of educational progress more closely resembles
> the flight of a butterfly than the flight of a bullet. (p. 167)

This was not only a useful insight for me, as it expressed what I knew to be true; it has come to be an extraordinarily valuable way of talking to policy analysts and legislators who fail to understand how much teaching resembles the flight of a butterfly and often want to create regulations and curriculum requirements that would make it into the flight of a bullet. There are also, of course, implications in this image of teaching for what teachers need to know and be able to do, to which I return later.

Jackson also wrote about the "multi-dimensionality and simultaneity" of teaching. I just *loved* that phrase. I went around for a couple of years just saying it, over and over again, in conversations and speeches and articles about teaching, because it captured for me what was missing from the research about teaching that I was encountering in the research world and from the view of teaching that many policymakers were adopting. Rarely does policy that would prescribe teachers' activities envision the dozens of experiences, activities, and goals that teachers must juggle all at once. Jackson eloquently resisted the technocratic views often propounded by those who do not teach. For many who have remote images of classrooms, students' experiences and interactions are not relevant to the teaching and learning process. All that matters is the text to be gotten through or the curriculum to be taught. This one-dimensional image has too often resulted in both research and policy that simplistically assume the key to teaching is to derive objective lists of content or procedures that can be marched through thoughtlessly or at least straightforwardly.

Around this time, I did a study with Arthur Wise at the RAND Corporation based in part on replicating interviews of teachers that he had conducted as a research assistant to Dan Lortie at the University of Chicago. (These were much of the data for Lortie's [1975] seminal work, *Schoolteacher.*) In this study, we talked to a large number of teachers about their experiences of educational policy. The teachers were the subject of top-down curriculum mandates in three separate school districts—well-intentioned policies that tried to improve teaching by specifying in more or less detail the precise content and procedures that teachers and students should go through. This was in the early 1980s during an era of competency-based education that sought to move children through various kinds of prescribed curricula—one of the many historical returns of the pendulum toward greater standardization in teaching.

The teachers saw that children's pathways to knowledge more resembled the flight of the butterfly than that of the bullet. They needed to start with the child to create connections between the child's understandings and experiences and the curriculum they wanted to teach. When we asked teachers what they considered first when planning their work, two-thirds mentioned students first, and almost all of the others mentioned students in the next breath, right behind curriculum goals (Darling-Hammond, 1996, pp. 72ff). Most teachers described their planning as starting with students and looping back to them while wending their way through many other concerns:

> First and foremost I think about what will interest these students and what they are familiar with that I can compare this new idea to: I start off with things they are familiar with and lead into the thing that is new to them. I also think about what their abilities are and what types of materials are available, then which of them the students would be most capable of handling. I try to get some variety into a lesson, perhaps changing activities two or three times during the course of the lesson to help connect with their interests. (pp. 73-74)

The teachers continually told us that the more thoroughly policymakers tried to prescribe the work of teaching, the less effective they could be in their work with children, because the hypothetical students who fit the prescriptions for practice on which those curricular systems were based represented few of the children they actually taught. They knew that to do their work they had to be free to chase butterflies—to follow the path of learning as it flitted throughout the classroom. They described a variety of ways that they sought to subvert the efforts of policymakers to control their teaching.

> I find myself playing a game at times, because when I am observed, I do what they are looking for. In the meantime, I still may be using techniques that I feel are best going to suit my students (p. 90).

> We have a set of guides that would just choke a horse. For instance, in one sub-area the material in the guide fills eight notebooks that are each 4 inches thick. . . . I say to the students, "These are the things that are identified in here. Now what are you particularly interested in?" And we make choices. Each of them picks out something they particularly like and they delve into that and report on it to the class. (p. 73)

But as rationalistic schemes for managing teaching took hold, most teachers felt that their views of good teaching were at odds with those of their school districts. While nearly 80% of teachers described concerns for children and for learning as central to good teaching, only 11% felt their school districts shared this view. Most (75%) felt their school districts were more concerned with implementing specific teaching techniques tied to precise objectives and with diagnosing student deficiencies. Teachers saw themselves as differing from their school districts in the extent to which they viewed students as active participants or passive recipients in the learning process, the extent to which they imagined student concerns as central or peripheral to the choice of learning goals and activities, and the extent to which they saw teaching as focused on student development or the identification of deficiencies. Many teachers felt that systems that marched students through the sequential testing of hundreds of discrete objectives missed the point of the learning process:

> Getting a kid interested in learning and keeping him interested is probably more important than doing checklists of goals and objectives on each kid for each content area. (p. 84)

> There is too much emphasis on "do this, do this, do this," rather than on the thinking process, which kids haven't learned, although they certainly have the ability. Not only is everything I'm supposed to cover prescribed for me, but there are tests given, so that if I felt I might take a little freedom (to focus on problem solving), there wasn't time. (p. 85)

> I am constantly being asked to define my goals, my way of achieving those goals, and my way of evaluating to see if I have achieved those goals. They seem to be very interested in that, and I get the impression that really is all they are interested in. But it couldn't be true. There must be some human beings up there (in the district office), too. (p. 84)

When we asked teachers whether there was anything that would make them consider leaving teaching, the single most frequent response had to do with the further bureaucratization of teaching—the imposition of additional constraints on what is taught and how:

> If they started tightening up any more as far as more testing, meeting more requirements . . . if it got any more standardized and routinized, if they told me that I couldn't do some of the things that I do in the way of interacting on a human level in the classroom, I would leave in a minute. (p. 91)

> If I can't be innovative and stay within the confines of the policy but use my own discretion and my own initiative . . . that would make me leave the school system. (p. 91)

> If they try to come in and force me to teach something that may not be applicable to my individual situation, then I would have to go back to something else. (p. 91)

I think if they dictated how I was going to teach every kid I might tell them goodbye. (p. 91)

Viewed against the images of teaching captured in *Life in Classrooms*, these teachers' words sound not petulant but wise. At some instinctive level they understood the conditions that must pertain for them to practice the art of student-responsive teaching that has a hope of success. Many teachers said they knew of others who had already left teaching because policies disabled them from teaching successfully. Detailed prescriptions for practice, it turns out, not only constrain teacher decision making, they also undermine the knowledge base of the profession and its ability to recruit and keep talented people. Professionally oriented teachers were those most troubled by edicts that ask them to focus on rules and reporting systems rather than on their students. As one explained:

I feel sorry for any teacher who is interested in teaching. It is going to be much worse in the years to come. For those who like the record keeping, and there are plenty of them—pathetic teachers but great record keepers—this will be a way of moving them up the ladder. It won't help the good teachers. It will help the people who teach by the book, because it is safe and it doesn't require any imagination. (p. 93)

Unfortunately, this sad situation has already come to pass in many districts, especially in urban communities that have imposed detailed, top-down curriculum prescriptions because they doubt (sometimes with reason) the competence of their teachers. Teachers' insistence on attending to students' experiences, interests, and prior knowledge were once thought to result from tenderheartedness and a disregard for "scientific" methods. Now, however, cognitive science has revealed that these considerations are essential, since learning is a process of making meaning out of new or unfamiliar events in light of familiar ideas or experiences. Learners construct knowledge as they build cognitive maps for organizing and interpreting new information. Effective teachers help students make these mental maps meaningful by drawing connections among different concepts and between new ideas and learners' prior experiences. Jackson's *Life in Classrooms* offered the detailed description of how teachers engage in this alchemy and supplied a key metaphor for our efforts to understand why, as Lee Shulman (1983) has said, "the juxtaposition of teaching and policy is the statement of a problem" (p. 488). It has also provided a text that generations of educators and researchers have used to develop a more genuine understanding of teaching and a more productive set of conceptual tools for helping teachers support learning.

Despite the appeal of the metaphor, however, it is not a given that teachers can ensure that the butterfly, in its flight, will land with the learning that is hoped to result. Teaching that balances the dialectic between children's experiences and interests and curriculum goals requires deep understanding of both students and subjects and a capacity to weave these together in ever-changing ways. Efforts to develop such thoughtful classrooms rely on substantial teacher knowledge and skill; indeed, they rely on a strong profession of teaching that helps teachers understand learning in all of its complexity and develop the skills to construct, recognize, and capitalize on the "teachable moment."

This problem is at the heart of the pendulum swings in policy from more complex, student-centered approaches and more standardized, teacher-proof initiatives. Lawrence Cremin (1965) argued that "progressive education . . . demanded infinitely skilled teachers, and it failed because such teachers could not be recruited in sufficient numbers" (p. 56). When educators who have been denied access to knowledge prove unable to manage complex forms of teaching, policymakers typically revert to simplistic prescriptions for practice, even though these cannot achieve the goals they seek. This is an even greater problem today than it might have been in times past, because the demands for higher-order thinking and performance from a much greater number of young people are acute, and the failure of society to meet these demands holds many greater dangers. Thus, it is important to dig deeper—to go beyond a vivid image of learning and teaching to an understanding of what it means to teach successfully at the intersection of students and subject matter.

TEACHING AS THE CULTIVATION OF EXPERIENCE

In the dialectic between the child and the curriculum (as Dewey framed it in his book by that title), the technocrat has often neglected the child. But progressives have been accused of neglecting the curriculum in this tension as well. Practice that succeeds in developing deep understanding of challenging content for a wide range of learners maintains a delicate balance between student and subject, allowing neither to overwhelm the other. The kind of nimble pedagogy that is suggested by this notion is what Philip Jackson has described so vividly in much of his writing. What his work has allowed many of us to do is to see what these abstractions look like in action, to understand what is meant by the need for improvisation on the part of teachers and also the need to understand the conditions of experience that might allow learners to move their understanding in deeper ways.

But how are teachers who are growing in their practice and teacher educators who are striving to develop such skillful teachers to figure out what to do? A second set of important insights about the resolution of this age-old dilemma is found in Jackson's response to Dewey's *Experience and Education*, published a few years ago by Kappa Delta Pi in a 60th anniversary edition of Dewey's work (Jackson, 1998a). As I wrote my own response to Dewey's piece for this volume, I not only found myself agreeing with Lee Shulman (Chapter 1, this volume) regarding Dewey's "anticipatory plagiarism," I also found, as has often been the case, that Phil's perceptiveness proved to be, in Dewey's words, educative. The images he developed regarding teaching as the cultivation of learning *within*, *by*, and *for* experience reveal more fully the meaning of Dewey's work and make it more applicable to our work today.

The issue that Dewey took up in *Experience and Education* was the battle between the traditionalists and the progressives. He foreshadowed the dance of the dichotomies we've seen continuously throughout the 20th century—the battles between phonics and whole language, for example, between "old" and "new" math, between direct instruction and discovery learning, between teacher-centered and student-centered pedagogies. Dewey noted:

> Mankind likes to think in terms of extreme opposites. It is given to formulating its beliefs in terms of *Either-Ors*, between which it recognizes no intermediate possibilities. . . . The history of educational theory is marked by opposition between the idea that education is development from within and that it is formation from without; that it is based upon natural endowments and that education is a process of overcoming natural inclination and substituting in its place habits acquired under external pressure. (LW.13.5)[1]

More than a half-century ago, Dewey urged the development of a more balanced educational philosophy—one forged through a thoughtful consideration of experience and its role in education, rather than by simplistic rejection of "old" ideas and the adoption of the opposite extreme. "Because the older education imposed the knowledge, methods, and the rules of conduct of the mature person upon the young, it does not follow, except upon the basis of the extreme *Either-Or* philosophy, that the knowledge and skill of the mature person has no directive value for the experience of the immature" (LW.13.8).

These words seem prescient as we consider how, for example, the idea of constructivism has been more recently misapprehended as a pedagogy that supposedly goes wherever the learner's own experience leads him, rather than as a fact about learning (it *is* constructed from learners' experiences, despite what other tacit assumptions might presume)—one that requires teachers to work with the learner's existing conceptions as well as the demands of the disciplines to shape an understanding of deeper principles and broader truths.

The critical issue in an education that seeks to make learning meaningful to the learner is to the ability of the teacher to forge *interactions* among students' impulses, curiosity, and prior knowledge and the subject matter under study: to bring it *into* experience, as Dewey suggests, rather than to assume that the learner's experience is irrelevant. At the same time, the teacher must be able to engage in curricular thinking, to develop the *continuity* of experience that adds up to understanding and that creates habits of mind. Thus, considerations of subject matter are combined with considerations of students. The teacher's role is not passive; instead, the teacher is extremely active in figuring out how to select material and construct experiences so that they connect to the interests and capacities of the learner and make future experiences more educative (Darling-Hammond, 1998). While the ideas of education "of, by, and for experience" (Dewey, LW.13.24) are resonant, however, it is not entirely clear what Dewey would have teachers actually *do* to achieve such educative interactions between students and subject matter.

The cryptic nature of Dewey's advice is part of what Jackson noted had annoyed him about *Experience and Education* when he first encountered it. In reflecting on why it was that the book had been bothersome to him, Phil realized that Dewey had packed into these very tightly packed aphorisms material that requires so much more thought and deliberation and understanding that at one point he talked about Dewey's advice as a collection of platitudes.

In beginning to deconstruct Dewey's words, Jackson clarified the critical role educators must play in planning for educative experiences for students, rather than just assuming that any old experience or child-initiated activity will automatically educate—the potentially fatal flaw of unthoughtful progressivism:

> What does it mean to offer such a challenge? All it says to me is that the reader or listener must work out on his or her own what it means to say that "education is a development within, by, and for experience." The truth is, however, that Dewey meant something very definite by each of those tiny prepositions, though he didn't pause to spell it out. When he said that education is a development *within* or *of* experience, he meant that not *all* of education is educative, only a portion of it is. The challenge to educators is to determine in advance what makes some experiences educative and others not. When he said that education is a development *by* experience, he meant that it is only *by means of* experience, by interacting with one's environment, that a person becomes educated. The challenge to educators is to design environments, chiefly in the form of classroom situations that actively engage the learner. But mere engagement, of course, is not enough. The educator must also assure that the form of engagement is *educative*. When he says that education is a development *for* experience, he means that the goal of education, its ultimate payoff, is not higher scores on this or that test, nor is it increased feelings of self-esteem or the development of psychological powers of this or that kind, nor is it preparation

for a future vocation. Instead, the true goal of education, Dewey wanted us to understand, is none other than richer and fuller *experiencing*, the ever-expanding capacity to appreciate more fully the living present. The challenge to educators is to translate that goal into reality, hour by hour, day by day, and subject by subject. (Jackson, 1998a, pp. 138–139; emphasis in original)

With these insights, we begin to develop an image of the teacher as a planner and, indeed, as a planter—someone who can anticipate productive starting points for the chasing of butterflies by arranging experiences and nurturing environments that, in the course of skillfully managed interactions, may enable students to benefit from the ideas they are encountering and develop the ability to continue to learn from their experiences. By considering the soil of the school, community, and classroom setting, as well as the individual organisms to be planted and nurtured—and by tending them daily in relation to their immediate and long-range needs and the goals of healthy growth—the teacher can cultivate conditions for learning. The process of bringing order to experience, of developing increasingly powerful explanations of things, is the process of developing disciplined understanding.

But the precise specifics of how to do this are not provided by Dewey, something Jackson (1998a) points out is a necessary frustration for educators:

The chief reason for the platitudinous advice, as I see it, laying aside the obvious constraints of time and the nature of the occasion, is that Dewey could not go much further than that on his own [to urge teachers and others to think about education by and through experience] without risking a different kind of disaster, caused by failing to take into account not just the background of the students with whom the teacher works but the specifics of the entire situation, which includes the material to be taught, the nature of the school as an institution, the social expectations impinging from the outside world, and much, much more. (p. 144)

All of these many factors that influence learning are at the core of the difficult task of preparing teachers to make sense of the buzzing, blooming confusion of classrooms. Indeed, I would argue they are the reasons why teachers must be prepared as professionals who are both deeply knowledgeable about how children learn and prepared to use many tools to support that learning—not as bureaucrats who are expected merely to implement a predetermined curriculum, often inappropriate to students' needs.

These many influences on the learner and his or her experience are also central to the challenge of preparing teachers to teach for social justice—that is, to teach in ways that are responsive to all of the learners they teach, including those whose backgrounds are very different from their own, whose experience bases are not the same as what they have come to understand through their own experience, and who live in a context where the social expectations Jackson references, which impinge from the outside world of the school and the society, are sometimes actually oppositional to the growth and aspirations of many young children.

How to prepare teachers to develop means for learning from the experiences of all of their students is a problem I have struggled with in teacher education. And in this essay, Jackson offers some additional images that have been extremely helpful to me in thinking about how to approach this dilemma. He points out that the difficulty in developing the kind of teaching Dewey described as reflecting the "new education" is that

> there seldom exists a one-to-one correspondence between a principle on the one hand and a practice on the other. What we find when we go looking case by case is that most principles lend support to multiple practices. Conversely, most practices draw upon more than a single principle. Moreover, the lines of influence that supposedly connect the two, fanning out, as they must do, from one to many and from many to one, are seldom the straight arrows that we find drawn on organizational charts. Instead, they more commonly resemble the irregular tracings left behind by a garden snail as it gingerly makes its way across the sidewalk's cruel cement or the back-and-forth trajectory of an autumn leaf as it slowly tacks to earth. There is something else to be said about those higgledy-piggledy lines, and it is this: the causal energies whose paths they graphically portray *flow in both directions at once.* (1998a, pp. 145-146; emphasis in original)

The image of the falling leaf tacking back and forth as it drifts to the ground is rather like the thought process teachers must go through as they think about individual children and consider generalizations about learning that might apply to a problem at hand, and then think again about the child and the extent to which the generalization may apply, and then recall another aspect of learning theory that may also be helpful in the explanation of what is seen in the classroom, and then consider what happened in a particular learning episode, and so on. This kind of restless, recursive thinking—from individual cases to broader principles and back again—is what teachers need to learn if they are to be truly responsive to their students' needs. A set of simple edicts for teaching—which are presumed somehow to be awaiting straightforward application to all students in all instances—will not suffice.

Jackson noted that a major point of Dewey's, one I had not completely absorbed previously, is that not only do principles affect practices, but practices also affect principles. "We learn," notes Jackson (1998a),

> from what we do, and the ripple effect of that learning reverberates from the periphery to the very core of our most treasured beliefs and values, which is

where things like principles and statements that express regularities of other kinds also reside. This doesn't mean that everything we believe in is up for grabs with each action we take. Some beliefs are more stable than others, thank heavens, which is why we name them premises, concepts, principles or even laws, rather than guesses or opinions or something else. [I would add grounded commitments as another source of stability.] But even the most stable of those constructions, Dewey would have insisted, remains open to the test of experience. (p. 146)

What this suggests is that, in addition to the importance of educating teachers for a complex world in which principles and practices are multiply reflected and determined, it is critical to educate them *within*, *by*, and *for* experience—a notion that suggests a reconceptualization of much of teacher preparation, a matter I discuss more below. In fact, just as students learn from their experience, teachers, too, learn from their experiences, and one of the most important things teacher educators can do is to construct educative experiences for prospective teachers that build upon what they understand, allow them to encounter new possibilities, and then enable them to reflect upon and learn from their experiences in ways that expand and transform the practice in which they engage.

One of the critical sites for learning *in* and *by* experience is, of course, the student teaching experience, along with its connections to coursework that frames the experience—a site that is often underexploited for developing strong and equitable teaching. Whereas many teacher education programs send candidates off to practice in classrooms chosen mostly because they are available, a much more transformative practice can result where programs take care to construct experiences that enable new teachers to work with experts who are knowledgeable, skillful, and committed to all of their students. If teachers learn *in* and *by* experience, they are unlikely to learn to teach well by imagining what good teaching might look like or by positing the opposite of what they have seen. In Stanford's Teacher Education Program, as in many others, we have recently overthrown the old expectations that abstract coursework can overcome the lessons of poor teaching models and have invested substantial effort not only in recruiting skilled and culturally responsive mentor teachers but also in developing professional development school relationships with schools that are working explicitly on an equity agenda. In these schools, novices can observe and participate in schooling that seeks to confront the long-standing barriers created by tracking, poor teaching, narrow curriculum, and unresponsive systems.

By shaping new teachers' evolving experiences of schooling and teaching, it is possible to construct a different foundation for learning to teach. However, more is needed to make these experiences productive of thoughtful action.

TEACHING AS REFLECTION AND MORAL ACTION

This point brings me to the third image of teaching I want to suggest, and that is teaching as the process of reflecting on the consequences of one's actions within a moral framework. The image is a contemplative one, but it is also a proactive one. If the teacher cultivates a nurturing environment and plants carefully considered experiences, considers what is transpiring as ideas take root and learning flits about, and seeks to understand the implications of these events for each child's learning and for the group as a whole, he or she must then use these insights to take action that creates ever more productive conditions for learning and growth. To explore what it means to learn to teach with such a reflective and moral stance, I want to take as a reference point *The Moral Life of Schools* (Jackson, Boostrom, & Hansen, 1993), and how it has helped me, and others, think about this task.

One of the powerful messages of *The Moral Life of Schools* is the recognition that, as the authors say, unintentional acts performed by teachers and administrators may have longer lasting effects than ones that are intentional or planned. If the challenge for teacher educators, especially those who aim to prepare socially conscious teachers, is to shape experiences for novices that allow them to understand more of the lives of their students as well as the consequences of their own actions, it is also to add to their ability productively to learn from those experiences—and to absorb the meaning of even unintentional acts of teaching.

How can one become alert to one's own acts, even the unintentional ones? As Jackson has asked, "Don't we all lose sight of the deeper significance of our actions from time to time?" Of course, we all do. How can we keep that significance before us and largely conscious? This is particularly salient with respect to teaching for social justice, because teaching in ways that are empowering for students whose experience is not only very different from one's own but also has been shaped by society to be restricted and, in many ways, oppressed, rests on becoming conscious of unintentional acts of both institutions and of teachers themselves.

Jackson and his colleagues call for autobiographical and reportorial work, including research by both scholars and teachers themselves, that addresses how teachers deal with the moral dilemmas that confront them. They also urge the adoption of a consciously sympathetic perspective—by both scholars and teachers—in observing, considering, and reporting on students and classrooms:

> To teach the whole child or the whole student, according to advocates of this position, is to take into consideration the student's feelings, attitudes, interests, and more. It is to think of each learner, in the degree to which it is possible to

do so, as an individual whose uniqueness calls for an individualized response from the teacher. . . . Like those who espouse a child-centered view, we too would urge that students be seen as individuals rather than as walking "brain boxes" or as statistical averages that exist only as abstractions. Moreover, the view we have taken makes clear what it means to look upon students (or anyone else) as individuals. It means stepping back from the rush of ongoing events, detaching ourselves from the immediacy of pedagogical demands at least long enough to begin to wonder what Ella or Lisa or Mr. Bailey or Richard is really like as a person. It also means taking into account our own feelings about that individual, and wondering why he or she makes us feel pleased or annoyed or simply puzzled and confused. It means, above all, being open to all that observation and reflection can reveal about that person while at the same time seeking to maintain a sympathetic frame of mind to encompass the growth of our understanding. (Jackson et al., 1993, pp. 275–276)

This cultivation of a sympathetic frame of mind is essential to the development of a morality that is relational and supportive rather than primarily judgmental. Jackson's insights have helped me to think about the work we do in teacher education programs in helping teachers learn to reflect on teaching and their roles as teachers through autobiographical and reportorial work, and in helping them to see from an empathetic perspective the lives of their students and to see their own work in that moral context.

Recently a group of students teachers and I developed a book entitled *Learning to Teach for Social Justice* (Darling-Hammond, French, & Garcia-Lopez, 2002), which emerged from the students' efforts, through the assignments and activities of the teacher education program and their own self-guided inquiry, to learn to teach in ways that are just and empowering for all of their students. They sought to examine how society constructs privilege and inequality and how this affects their own opportunities as well as those of others; to see themselves in relation to others; to explore their own students' experiences and appreciate how these experiences had informed different worldviews, perspectives, and opportunities; and to evaluate how life in classrooms operates and how it can be structured to enable learning for all students. Their efforts were to develop the kind of "equity pedagogy" James Banks (1993) talks about, built on awareness combined with knowledge about how different children learn and how various teaching strategies can productively engage children who learn in distinctive ways.

The primary learning strategies of these young teachers were the close observation of life in schools and classrooms coupled with collegial reflection that raised and pursued searching questions. Supported by the many case studies and research projects embedded in their teacher education program, the student teachers undertook several kinds of inquiries—regarding students, classroom events, and school contexts—to help themselves consider the moral implications of life in classrooms. They shared this work with each other, and they organized conversations to engage one another in a concerted effort to probe its meanings.

Lee Shulman (Chapter 1, this volume) notes that one of the things we learn from Jackson's work is that the longer and more carefully we look at something, the more we care for it. This phenomenon was certainly evident in this student-initiated working group on social justice. Indeed, this recognition forms the rationale for a pedagogy in teacher education in which teachers conduct child case studies, look deeply at the lives of children, look deeply at life in classrooms, and conduct inquiries within communities and schools, in large part to develop the capacity to understand and to care. To see students in another way, to look at and listen carefully and nonjudgmentally to students to uncover who they really are and what they think, is a central theme of Jackson's work.

It is also a theme of Paulo Freire, whom I read in dialogue with Phil. Friere (1998) talks about the importance of preparing teachers for "reading" a class of students as if it were a text to be decoded and comprehended, especially when teachers come from economic and cultural backgrounds substantially different from those of their students. He argues:

> Just as in order to read texts we need auxiliary tools such as dictionaries or encyclopedias, the reading of class as texts also requires tools that can be easily used. It is necessary, for example, to *observe* well, to *compare* well, to *infer* well, to *imagine* well, to *free one's sensibilities* well, and to believe in others without believing too much what one may think about others. One must exercise one's ability to *observe* by recording what is observed, but recording should not be limited to the dutiful description of what takes place from one's own perspective. It also implies taking the risk of making critical and evaluative observations without giving such observations the air of certainty. All such material should be in constant analysis by the teacher who produces it, as well as by his or her students. (p. 49; emphasis in original)

The importance of ongoing, careful observation and analysis returns us to the notion that preparation for teaching means learning to learn from experience and to consider experience through a lens that gives honor to the human beings who are in the teacher's care—perhaps the most important aspect of a moral profession based on both knowing and caring. As Jackson and colleagues (1993) note in *The Moral Life of Schools*, the teacher's and the child's reality is shaped by how a teacher learns to look and think about individual students and their relationship:

> Once a teacher, for example, perceives one of her students as begin sullen and untrustworthy, once she describes him to herself in those terms, her reality (i.e.

The Class opening scene

> the field of forces to which she accommodates as she goes about the job of teaching) has undergone a significant change and so has the reality of the student who has been so judged (i.e. *his* reality now contains a teacher who perceives him in that way), although he may never recognize that to be so. However, though perceptions may be real functionally, they still may be unwarranted or underserved, which is where prolonged observation and reflection become helpful if not indispensable. . . . It often happens that the more we look and the longer we reflect on what we have seen, the more complicated the perceived object, scene, or person seems to become and the more we are led to reject simplistic interpretations of its meaning or significance. (pp. 273–274; emphasis in original)

Jackson's work reminds us constantly of the importance of learning to see in a way that enables both caring and the use of teaching knowledge and skills, drawing upon a moral commitment to find a way to honor and work with every child. This merger of knowledge and caring is crucial to a moral profession. In recent years, for example, we have all heard the slogan repeatedly that "all children can learn," and many advocates have exhorted teachers to believe that all children can learn. But, even if they are inclined to adopt this worldview, teachers find it impossible to continue to believe that all children can learn if they don't have skills, tools, and strategies to enable them to learn. Sooner or later, if a teacher has only a slogan and good intentions, but lacks the knowledge of how children learn and what they need, students will fail to learn, and the instinct will be to blame them, rather than to inquire into one's own actions.

Teachers must have the opportunity to ask and seek answers to the hard questions they struggle with in forging knowledgeable and caring relationships with their students. One example of the process of inquiry leading to broader learning is reflected in a student teacher's chapter for the book on *Learning to Teach for Social Justice* (Darling-Hammond et al., 2002), which she entitled, "Can White Teachers Effectively Teach Students of Color?" This young teacher recounted how an assignment in her teacher education program that asked her to characterize her own identity sensitized her to the possibilities of stereotyping and the social consequences of labeling. And she noted how sharing her colleagues' insights and stories brought her insights about her own experiences and goals as a teacher. She wrote: "As we discussed teaching for diversity at STEP, I wondered, how was I affecting my students' lives? Had I created a safe learning environment for them? Was I showing my students respect for their cultures, their individuality?" (p. 46).

Asking these kinds of questions is the beginning of a process of reflection about one's identity as a teacher and as a moral being that, once begun, is not easily stopped. This young teacher decided to conduct a student survey in the high school where she was student teaching about what students felt it took for them to learn from a teacher, exploring in particular their perceptions of the importance of race in shaping their experiences and their views of teachers. She learned that race was not what students largely responded to in their teachers, but that empathy, fairness, and willingness to assist learning were extremely important to them. As she shared these findings with the other student teachers with whom she was studying, their ensuing dialogue inspired them to examine their own acts as teachers. Their conversation, like many others that were part of this process, constructed a space for the sharing of perspectives in support of moral as well as technical learning.

The capacity for perspective-taking that develops through participation in a community in which diverse experiences and views are elicited and shared is one of the things we're reminded of throughout Jackson's work. He illustrates in both his observations and his methods how teachers' efforts to construct many opportunities for students (and for each other) to share what they think and what they know becomes part of the heart of the *educative* process, that is, the process of constructing new experiences on which people can learn to learn *from* experience, pursued as butterflies, not bullets. In teacher education programs, as in other settings, the use of the group as an educative body requires skillful management of discussions that can often result in the assertion of one view or one set of experiences over another and careful attention to the questions of standing, entitlement, and voice in the group. Jackson has been able to help us think about how that might occur by considering how students and teachers interact in classrooms, as well as how teachers interact with each other—and even with researchers—in making sense of their work. As noted in *The Moral Life of Schools* (Jackson et al., 1993):

> Beyond extending their naturally sympathetic view to take in everything they see and hear, which includes themselves, teachers who want to explore the expressive meaning of their environment to its fullest need to make a special effort to *say* what they see and think. They need to put into words their hunches and suspicions, their doubts and budding convictions, no matter how tentatively held or crudely phrased such premonitions and intuitions may turn out to be. (p. 263; emphasis in original)

The journey toward deeper understandings of one's work and one's purposes is intensely personal, and yet it is necessarily also social. It has to be conducted in the company of others who can teach us about their own experiences and who learn with us about how to build a common understanding that's greater than the sum of its parts. In *Democracy and Education*, John Dewey noted that "a democracy is more than a form of government; it is primarily a mode of associated living" (MW.9.93). He stressed the importance of creating circumstances in which people participate in a growing number of associations with others, noting that:

> In order to have a large number of values in common, all the members of the group must have an equitable opportunity to receive and to take from others. There must be a large variety of shared undertakings and experiences. Otherwise, the influences that educate some into masters educate others into slaves. And the experience of each party loses in meaning. (MW.9.90)

To be educative, schools must consciously create community from the sharing of multiple perspectives. Finding space for reflection and discourse about who we are, individually and collectively, in relation to one another and to society at large creates the initial foundation for all the other necessary work on social justice. One of the things both Dewey's and Jackson's ideas have meant for me as a teacher educator is the importance of creating spaces for associated living with a very diverse group of prospective teachers. About half of the candidates in Stanford's Teacher Education Program are students of color, and all of the students in the program have different life experiences. But finding ways that those experiences can be shared—in such ways that all of the participants feel they have a voice and standing to learn from each other—is, as anyone who does this kind of work knows, an extremely delicate business. And the construction of conversations in a public space created for sharing those multiple perspectives is one of the first moral tasks of a teacher education program and the continuing job of schools.

IMAGES OF PHILIP JACKSON AND HIS WORK

Because I have tapped Dewey repeatedly in reflecting on Phil Jackson's work (and Jackson in reflecting on Dewey's), I want to close with some words *by* John Dewey—the anticipatory plagiarist was also, I believe, an anticipatory memoirist—*about* Philip Jackson and some words by Phil Jackson about John Dewey (which are really, I think, about Philip Jackson). Dewey noted:

> There is an old saying to the effect that it is not enough for a man to be good; he must be good for something. The something for which a man must be good is the capacity to live as a social member so that what he gets from living with others balances with what he contributes. What he gets and gives as a human being, a being with desires, emotions, and ideas, is not external possessions, but a widening and deepening of conscious life—a more intense, disciplined, and expanding realization of meanings. . . . To maintain capacity for such education is the essence of morals, for conscious life is a continual beginning afresh. . . . Interest in learning from all contacts of life is the essential moral interest. (MW.9.369, 370)

I think that Dewey had Philip Jackson in mind when he penned those words!

This is what Jackson (1998a) said about Dewey, and when I read it, it seemed to me that it was really about Jackson himself, though he didn't mean it that way:

> Dewey's way of inspiring was not to set forth a vision for others to realize. Not even his laboratory school was intended to do that. His way was the way of inquiry. It was to invite thought, to insist upon it, to engage in it himself openly and responsibly, sometimes even torturously, I have to say. His way was to trust that such thought, even when labored and haltingly expressed, can in the long run only lead to wiser actions and better practices than would have occurred without it. (p. 148)

Philip Jackson's work has, for me and for many others, led to wiser action and better practices than would have been the case otherwise. And for this we thank him deeply.

On Seeing the Moral
in Teaching

David T. Hansen

S EEING IS metamorphosis, not mechanism," writes James Elkins (1996). "It alters the thing that is seen and transforms the seer" (p. 12).

Elkins's claim, to which I will return throughout this essay, suggests that seeing as a human experience constitutes more than the biochemical operations of the eye, just as photography as an art involves more than the mechanical operations of the camera. Seeing denotes the transformation of a thing into an object; for example, a four-limbed moving creature becomes what we call a person, an oddly shaped thing becomes a stone, a mass of white stuff becomes a cloud, a peculiar set of markings becomes written language, and so on ad infinitum. From the moment people are born into culture and language, they engage in this transforming process. As they mature, it becomes instantaneous, like the speed of light, and taken for granted, like the act of breathing.

Elkins takes care to distinguish perception from fantasy. He is not suggesting people can see whatever they feel like seeing. The term *metamorphosis* embodies the continuity between thing and object, between the inchoate, endlessly varied stuff of the world and its transformation into identifiable, meaningful objects such as persons, stones, clouds, and books. Elkins also calls attention to the reciprocal effect the transformative process has on the perceiver. For example, from the very instant that I am introduced to the person who works in the office next to me, I *see* that person as a colleague, as a potential supporter or rival, as a possible friend, as a fellow sojourner, and any number of other possibilities. This seeing has now altered my world and me, however subtly. To take another example, the very instant that I see for the first time a cell divide under a microscope, I perceive things differently than before. In short, the world in which persons dwell is a scene of endless metamorphoses.

Elkins's claim has a familiar ring today among those who do qualitative educational research. It calls to mind the widespread criticism of positivism that, over the last few decades, has jarred that approach to social inquiry off its pedestal. Researchers today strive to be more sensitive than hitherto to how their ways of seeing affect the objects of inquiry, and vice versa (cf. Tyack, 1997). Many conduct their work mindful of how the very act of perception compromises the presupposition that coming to know something boils down to aligning our "inner" mental representations with "outer" reality—an assumption that, in turn, presumes there is a pure ontological distinction between the subject (the perceiver) and the object (the perceived). Thanks to the influence of philosophers as diverse as John Dewey, Michel Foucault, Hans-Georg Gadamer, and Ludwig Wittgenstein, many scholars today treat the relation between the researcher and the researched as more complicated than the purified categories of positivism allow (Phillips & Burbules, 2000).

This "interpretive turn" in social inquiry, as Paul Rabinow and William Sullivan (1979) termed it in a widely influential book, was well underway in the late 1980s when I was a doctoral student at the University of Chicago. My dissertation adviser, Philip Jackson, was attuned to the sea change. He was familiar with what Clifford Geertz (1983) called the emergence of "blurred genres" in the social sciences (cf. Jackson, 1990a). Moreover, he had himself already made the turn from a positivist orientation to an interpretive approach in studying educational practice (cf. Jackson, 1990b). I understand better now, with the benefit of hindsight, how profoundly these transformations influenced the substance and style of the guidance Jackson provided me. As a qualitative researcher, he was extraordinarily attentive to everyday human actions and doings. His method of working embodied a vivid example of the value in pondering mechanism and metamorphosis in how one perceives the world. Indirectly, his approach also opened up considerable space for me to develop my own methods of inquiry. In that space, which feels ever expanding, I learned how to regard teaching in ways that I have found enduringly productive and meaningful. In this essay, I will describe the origins of this outcome.

FIELDWORK AS EDUCATIVE

I worked with Jackson as a research assistant on the Moral Life of Schools Project, a 3-year study (1988–1990) funded by the Spencer Foundation. Robert Boostrom (now at the University of Southern Indiana and a contributor to this volume) was the other research assistant on the project. Eighteen teachers also participated, nine from three elementary schools (one public, one Catholic, one independent) and nine from three secondary schools (also public, Catholic, and independent). Over the course of the project, we all met as a group every 2 weeks for dinner and conversation about moral aspects of teaching and schooling. We three researchers also observed hundreds of classes. I concentrated on the high schools, as well as a few middle grades, and observed over 400 classes taught by our colleagues working at those levels (for further details, see Boostrom, Hansen, & Jackson, 1993; Hansen, 1995; Jackson, Boostrom, & Hansen, 1993).

Jackson, Boostrom, and I met at least once every week in Jackson's office to discuss our observations and other matters pertaining to the project. His typical way of opening a meeting, as I recall it, was to ask: What did you see? or How should we begin? Once somebody had put something forward for consideration, we would explore its possible meanings and ramifications. We would pursue whatever direction the conversation took and would keep going until it was time to stop talking and leave. I do not recall a single instance in which Jackson told me what to look for in the schools and classrooms. Nor to my recollection did he ever inform or guide me in *how* to look. Neither in our very first meeting nor in our final one years later did Jackson ever put forth an observational schedule or a list of things to count or check off while observing. He did not oblige me to read any particular books or articles about qualitative research. Moreover, none of the courses I had taken with him up to that point included any readings about methodology in social inquiry.

I do not recall a single instance in the history of the project when Jackson offered directives or guidance about validity, inter-rater reliability, generalizability, variables, hypotheses, research design, and so forth. According to many perspectives, these terms constitute the bread and butter of good research practice. Since I had read a range of works on research methodology, either on my own or in other courses, I remember sensing that Jackson's orientation was, shall I say, unusual. And yet his entire presence as a teacher and adviser was unusual. I would call it Socratic: a way of working in which questioning, doubting, and wondering are key elements and in which the student never quite knows the teacher's own conclusions and convictions. The teacher's elusiveness combined with sustained inquiry into the subject matter at hand can generate a productive tension that, in turn, fuels the passion to learn (I've sought to capture the profound influence Jackson as teacher had on me in Hansen, 1996). Socrates talked a lot, however, and Jackson's posture also involved silence and contemplation, as if to speak about something too hastily (or confidently) would puncture it like a balloon. It would diminish or even trivialize the object in view.

I do not mean to suggest that Jackson disregarded or disdained the concerns that underlie the familiar vocabulary of validity, reliability, and generalizability. Quite the contrary. I was struck by how determined he was to pursue whatever interested him in his fieldwork and by how open-minded he was about adopting standpoints, ideas, and methods that would help him. Nor am I presuming here to capture Jackson's approach to research, which he has articulated himself (e.g., Jackson, 1992a). Rather, what stands out for me now is the *experience* his orientation made possible for me. In the extensive classroom and school visits I undertook during those years, I was able to enact and cultivate all the powers of perception, attunement, and insight I had managed willy-nilly to develop up to that point as a human being and as an inquirer. I appreciate more and more what it has meant to me, as a scholar, to have been provided the time and space in my doctoral research to draw upon whatever powers of perception I had as a person—not just some of them, predetermined by a prior checklist of things to look for, but *all* of them. This experience was made possible by the steady, everyday example of Jackson's scholarly focus, tenacity, and integrity.

The fieldwork, for me, was an opportunity in the richest sense of that term. It was rewarding to develop my own relationship with our colleagues from the schools I was regularly visiting. I relished the liberty to establish my own schedule of classroom observations in coordination with what the teachers were up to and to work out and test my own conjectures, interpretations, and, eventually, arguments, with helpful and timely input from Jackson, Boostrom, and several of the teachers. The schools, the classrooms, the teachers, the students, the curriculum, and so much more differed in striking and provocative ways. The task of making sense of these things proved to be intense, demanding, incredibly time-consuming, fascinating, and sometimes inspiring. During those years I lived and breathed the project. My dreams at night were often filled with images emanating from what I heard and witnessed.

I visited one or another of the schools almost every day of the week and also attended weekend activities such as sporting events. I sat in on the nine middle and high school teachers' classes regularly, although in no lockstep sequence or order. I would observe one or more of a particular teacher's classes for several days in a row, in order to develop a feel for rhythm and flow. I always tried to reach class before a school period was scheduled to start. If I arrived late, even a minute after a lesson had begun, I usually walked away without making my presence known and would head to the school library or cafeteria to wait out the period—or dash to the car and drive to another school. I followed this practice because I did not want to interrupt classes in progress and because I preferred observing them in their entirety. Often I was the first person who entered the classroom. I always sat at the back or side of a room and sought to remain as unnoticeable as possible. As lessons proceeded, I avoided eye contact with teacher and students and tried to appear emotionally uninvolved with what was occurring. I spoke with individuals during class time only if they spoke to me.

I acted this way because I did not want to influence the classrooms any more than was inevitable. I learned to concentrate intently on observing the proceedings. In time, I became so immersed in the process that I was invariably thrown into confusion when someone, usually the teacher, did happen to address me during class. To employ Elkins's terms, those moments ruptured the organic transaction between seer and seen.

For example, one morning in March one of the teachers and his students were discussing Indira Ghandi's career as a political leader. The question arose whether she was related to Mahatma Ghandi. No one knew. Suddenly, the teacher looked over and asked me if I knew. Thoroughly startled, I sputtered that I could not say. My inability to state something I had actually known for a long time may have been a result of sudden nervousness, but I believe it stemmed from my utter absorption in *taking in*, in the literal sense of the term, the life of the classroom.

To consider a second instance, one morning in April a science teacher was discussing with her students a recent incident in which a student from another class had poured acid on the belongings of a classmate. After expressing her displeasure with the act, as well as her concern for the boy whose things were damaged, she asked students what should be done about it. In the midst of their discussion she suddenly turned to me and said, "Perhaps Mr. Hansen could talk to us about this." Startled out of my observational mode, I walked to the front and posed a few questions about how students felt about the incident. I was met with curious looks and blank stares, as if these seventh graders were thinking "Well, well, this guy who's been hanging out all this time can actually talk." Very quickly, and in a natural and matter-of-fact way, the teacher elbowed me aside, retook the reins, and urged her students to think about an appropriate sanction and to remember how important it is to respect one another's property and person. I slunk back to my seat, relieved to be out of the spotlight.

The incident occurred in the fourth month of the project, a time when the teachers and researchers were still becoming acquainted as participants. Just as I had a great deal still to learn about the teachers and their work, so they did not yet perceive what I was doing in their classrooms. *I did not either*. In keeping with the project's focus, I was interested in the everyday moral dimensions of what goes on in classrooms and schools. But I did not know how these dimensions would manifest themselves, nor even how to characterize them (despite or perhaps because of being reasonably well versed in moral philosophy). I was attuned to familiar "moral" things such as how the teachers and students regarded and treated one another. But I was not applying a preset moral theory that would help me categorize those things, nor was I testing a hypothesis. I did not understand at the start of the project how to formulate a moral framework on teaching that would respect, at one and the same time, broad educational values and the unrepeatable particulars of teaching as a complicated, dynamic human practice. (I am still working on this task, for me a scholarly version of pursuing the Holy Grail.) It was troubling and at times embarrassing not to be able to offer the teachers a clear, straightforward account of what I was only slowly, and in a piecemeal way, coming to identify. In those early months, things were so uncertain that the science teacher simply assumed I must be a professional ethicist or moral authority, somebody who could offer her and her students superior expertise on matters of right and wrong.

Jackson had shared with Boostrom and me the proposal that had secured funding for the project, which outlined in general terms the experimental, open-ended, and long-term nature of the inquiry. The proposal did not specify what phenomena would be the focus nor what framework of analysis would be deployed to interpret them. In keeping with this approach, just as Jackson did not offer observational checklists, so he did not impose a particular meaning or framework on the moral. Although my memory may be playing tricks here, it seems to me he actually steered our talk *away* from moral theories and philosophies, concentrating instead on our own observational reactions and speculation. We developed a habit of sharing conjectures about the possible significance of what we were witnessing. Following Jackson's example, I learned to draw upon my reading in philosophy, anthropology, and other disciplines, as well as upon fiction, poetry, film, and more.

During one of our evening meetings in June, toward the close of that first year of the project, several teachers expressed a feeling of being "left hanging" because they did not know what I was "finding out" in their classrooms. They said they felt uncomfortable. The rest of the group sympathized. Particularly since our project's focus was on the *moral* life of schools, it was natural that the teachers might feel they were being judged. And so they were, albeit not in ways they might initially have imagined, nor in ways that I could have articulated at the time. At this meeting, I responded to their concerns by saying that I was still trying to make sense of the moral import of the everyday exchanges and routines I was witnessing. I explained that I was not zeroing in on disputes, dilemmas, and other dramatic events or issues that are the usual focus when the topic of the moral comes up (and that many of our evening conversations had pivoted around). But I could not be more specific. I simply did not know how to be. I recall *feeling* that the intensity of my daily observations and conversations was having an effect. It was shaping "the seer and the seen," as Elkins might put it, but I had no language for capturing that effect. Nor did Jackson or Boostrom proffer such a language. Each was pursuing his own particular interests related to the moral, which also centered around the everyday world of the classroom.

Over the ensuing summer, I wrote a paper on the moral significance of classroom beginnings, those few minutes when teacher and students prepare themselves for the day's lesson (Hansen, 1989). Jackson offered invaluable suggestions and ideas on this paper, my first as a qualitative researcher. The theme of the paper emerged from systematically reading the pile of notes I had written based on my fieldwork (see below). Over the months of observing, I had become increasingly aware of how productive some of the teachers' classes were. More and more, these classes struck me as purposeful and engaging. Reading my collected notes, as if they constituted a text in their own right, taught me that one reason for that feeling of purposefulness was that the teachers and their students got down to business in short order after the bell. They did not dawdle, shuffle papers, goof around, or otherwise waste time. They took out materials, pens, books, and anything else they might need even as they took their seats and finished off conversations. In a nutshell, I could see in my notes repeated evidence for the fact that the teachers cared about their work. They seemed to take advantage of every minute they had with their students.

I centered the paper around three of the teachers' classrooms, and I shared it with the whole group. These actions seemed to help break the ice. It was not so much that the teachers I was working most closely with could now say, in effect, "Oh, so that's what you're paying attention to." It was more a matter of dissolving lingering ambiguities and anxieties, of simply being able to share, finally, a concrete example of what I was perceiving. From the very first second I had stepped into their classrooms, the teachers had been making visible their ways of seeing. Now I was able to make visible to them aspects of my own.

In due course, the teachers and I developed a shared approach to the project. We treated the whole affair as an inquiry, in which each of us could pursue issues, questions, and themes of particular interest. The teachers came to see that my role was not to judge how "good" or "bad" they were as educators. (Of course, I had indicated this from the start, but once more the term *moral* in itself seemed to render suspect any disclaimers.) Nor was my role to offer tips and techniques on how to render their practice "more moral."

This outcome resulted, in part, from sharing my paper, but much more so from just being together more and more: at the biweekly dinners and, above all, at lunch and at other breaks during the schoolday when I was visiting. From the beginning of the project, I had made it a habit to spend time with the teachers after observing their classes and would talk for as long as their schedules permitted.

During the second year of fieldwork, the teachers had become so used to my visits that, according to their testimony as well as my own observations, they took my presence in stride. We also talked more and more, although not in so many words, about our various ways of perceiving the world. For example, one of the teachers asked me at one of our evening gatherings that second year whether I thought she had changed as a teacher. She explained that she herself was unsure about the matter, even though the project had been stimulating her to think in new ways about her work and about what it meant to be a teacher. I responded that I was seeing new things in her practice but that I wasn't sure whether this fact meant that *she* had changed or whether it signaled a change in *me*, such that I could now see what was always there but did not have eyes for before.

For me, the ability to talk with the teachers in more comfortable and inquiry-oriented terms resulted not only from our lengthy time together but also from the extensive writing I did throughout the project. I took notes regularly while observing. I would jot down words or phrases as certain events and activities took place. At other times, I wrote rapidly in order to capture dialogue or to record the precise sequence of doings. I kept track of the range of activities undertaken during a class and how much time was devoted to them. That focus resulted, in part, from the general orientation toward the everyday mentioned above. It also expressed, in retrospect, the fact that I had spent years at a previous job observing teachers who were learning how to lead classroom discussions and offering them highly detailed feedback. Thus, I was drawing, in part, on habit (more on this below). There were also stretches of time during which I simply watched and listened. Later in the day, after school was over, I would convert these field notes into longer notes, describing activities at length and generating questions and provisional interpretations. My wife and I had a fireplace in our apartment, and during the long Chicago winters I would return from my fieldwork, light a fire, and write for hours and hours.

In the first year and a half of the project, when I did the bulk of my observational work, I took about 1,300 pages of field notes in 4-by-6 notebooks. I also recorded many hours of comments on a pocket tape recorder I kept in my car, which I would talk into while particular scenes were still vivid. I converted these notes and recordings into over 600 8½-by-11 pages of notes for reference use. I organized the notes by teacher, by individual class, and by the timing during class when particular acts took place. I numbered and dated the notes sequentially. I described activities in narrative form and sometimes interwove lengthy working interpretations. I kept separate files for each school, organizing sequentially and by type the many school events and activities I witnessed. I also developed an annotated bibliography of what I read during the course of the project, including scholarly works in philosophy and social science, as well as novels and poetry. Finally, I kept a file that recorded dreams and other diverse reflections having to do with the project.

The upshot of all this observing, talking, and writing was a perspective both on teaching and on how to study it that has served me through the present day. Although I had done some school teaching before, and had also worked with many, many teachers in other professional capacities, I learned more about the practice of teaching in this project than from all of those experiences combined. That outcome was a function of the longitudinal nature of the project, of the insight of my dissertation adviser Jackson and my peer Boostrom, and of spending so much time with a group of remarkable teachers. Moved especially by Jackson's ever-present example, I learned a great deal about how to attend to and respect the ordinary, the everyday, and the apparently humdrum and routine in classroom life. I learned to see the moral significance of classroom beginnings and of other ritualized aspects of how teachers and students work. I discerned the layers of moral meaning embedded in a group's habits of turn-taking. I witnessed how morally expressive a teacher's everyday style of interacting with students and the curriculum can be. I had the time to observe intensively particular classes over an entire schoolyear and to see how a teacher and students together can fashion a moral community: a set of shared expectations, norms, values, and ways of acting that create an environment in which teaching and learning come into being, in the most literal sense of those terms.

The structure of the project—or, better perhaps, the absence of a preset structure—positioned me to draw fully on the ways of perceiving, thinking, and feeling that I had developed up to that point in my life. As I learned how to see and to think about the moral dimensions of teaching, I also learned how to see and to think about my own education as a human being. Phrased differently, I learned something about myself as "an instrument" of inquiry—the perceiver—at precisely the same moment that I was learning how to see the moral in teaching—the perceived.

PERCEPTION AND METAMORPHOSIS

As a boy I had lived for some years in Pakistan and Nigeria, with their widely different cultural customs and environmental settings. As an American, being thrown into these worlds compelled me to expand my horizons of perception. The schools I attended had the same impact. They featured teachers from all over the world, and there were children from near and far as well. The schools' rituals and routines differed markedly from what I was used to in the United States, as did some of the teachers' styles. I remember a teacher, who was from England, angrily shouting at a Nigerian boy, "Don't say 'What?' to me— that's what Americans do!" I recall another teacher, also from England, who spent hours after school teaching me the multiplication tables so I could catch up with other pupils. I studied the history of Britain and knew its kings and queens before I had ever cracked a textbook on American history. Like the other pupils, at my wooden desk I used an old-style pen that had to be dipped continually in an inkwell, a messy process (I went through countless sheets of blotting paper) that links me more with my grandparents than with today's children.

A difficult feature of these and other moves while in grades K–12 was being wrenched from one group of friends and suddenly parachuted into a strange, distant world where things had to start all over again (these were the days before e-mail). That sometimes traumatic experience also compelled me to push my horizons of perception, if only because I could not presume (nor could I put into words at the time) what Jackson (1986) calls "the presumption of shared identity." I learned something about being a reader of subtle human cues in order to tune into the cultural ethos. To echo a metaphor from Clifford Geertz, a person who wants to find his feet in a new setting had better attend to nuance and detail.

Another consequence of these journeys was discovering the endless possibilities of solitude. (Are those possibilities waning today because of e-mail?) I spent a lot of time on my own, especially before meeting new chums to hang around with, but also out of habit. The poet Friedrich Holderlin (1990, p. 13) evokes the promise of solitude in his poem "When I Was a Boy":

When I was a boy
  A god often rescued me
    From the shouts and the rods of men
      And I played among trees and flowers
       Secure in their kindness
        And the breezes of heaven
         Were playing there too.

And as you delight
The hearts of plants
When they stretch towards you
With little strength

So you delighted the heart in me
Father Helios, and like Endymion
I was your favorite,
Moon. O all

You friendly
And faithful gods
I wish you could know
How my soul has loved you.

Even though when I called to you then
It was not yet with names, and you
Never named me as people do
As though they knew one another

I knew you better
Than I have ever known them.
I understood the stillness above the sky
But never the words of men.

Trees were my teachers
Melodious trees
And I learned to love
Among flowers.

I grew up in the arms of the gods.

Holderlin makes plain that solitude does not mean being solitary, like an atom in the void. He speaks of learning to respond to the voice of nature, endowed here with a beneficent intent infused into it, in turn, from the "friendly and faithful gods" whose presence mirrors back to the boy his sense of homage. Nature and the gods have been his moral educators, teaching him how to love even before he had the "names," the language, to describe his education. Now he does have language. He is a poet with the words to sketch the scene of his most fundamental instruction as a human being. That instruction was not in customary knowledge and information, all "the words of men" that he could not understand, perhaps because they were shouted at him, they were not "melodious," they were coercive (accompanied by the rod) rather than invitational. Rather, the knowledge he gained was the grace of gratitude for being, and he sings to his primordial teachers. He holds them in his arms, which are the lines of his poem.

The encompassing sense of gratitude that Holderlin describes can emerge from the experience of solitude, understood as distinct from a state of exile, loneliness, or isolation. The experience is one of pulsing in the very lap of life. I part company with Holderlin in only one aspect. Though I was a migrant from one school to another as a boy, I do not recall the feeling of alienation from human institutions that Holderlin also evokes. Perhaps most of us *suffer* school (though some relish it); we learn to accept it, endure it, manage in it, even survive it. With its brick and mortar and bells and shouts, school is anything but a field of trees and flowers. Solitude can be hard to find within its walls; it is easier to be solitary. "How much more appropriate to strew classrooms with leaf and flower than with blood-stained birch-rods," wrote Michel de Montaigne. "I would have portraits of Happiness there and Joy, with Flora and the Graces" (Montaigne, 1592/1991, p. 186). Moreover, as Tom James writes (Chapter 7, this volume), school teaches many of us what William Golding portrayed in harrowing fashion in his *Lord of the Flies*—that children thrown together in school or elsewhere can bring considerable pain to one another.

But there is another side. For me schooling's moral impact was not entirely problematic, not solely a matter, for instance, of learning to fabricate a public mask in order to hide private daydreams, musings, and yearnings. As rough-and-tumble as school was at times, I think I was fortunate to be surrounded day after day during those years by children from literally hither and yon. I learned a great deal about how to observe, adapt, play, and talk.

While working in the Moral Life of Schools Project years later, I saw that my education both in and outside of school had been a process, at least in part, of learning how to pay attention to the everyday and the apparently ordinary. I realized this was a habit in which I was at home, whether it involves staring out a bus window, walking along a forest path, watching a niece or nephew at play, sitting in the stands at a local basketball game where you don't know anybody—or hanging out in the back of an unfamiliar classroom. The fact I became so swiftly absorbed in my school and classroom observations during the project, and equally invested in the solitude of writing and reflection, reminded me that I was bound to the human tapestry that is always before us if we have eyes to see, if we're willing to accept the metamorphoses to which Elkins refers.

The sense of gratitude to the scenes of one's instruction can become sentimental and obfuscate the fact that it depends on a sense of obligation. The painter Paul Cezanne provides a helpful perspective on how to step back from the sentimental and the consoling, and to remember that seeing the world is not fantasizing about it but rather is being attentive to it. He says this about his artistic hopes: "A minute in the world's life passes! To paint it in its reality! And forget everything for that. *To become that minute, be the sensitive plate, . . . give the image of what we see*, forgetting everything that has appeared before our time" (quoted in Merleau-Ponty, 1964, p. 169; emphasis in original).

Cezanne's passionate ambition mirrors an ideal of qualitative research with its interest in "qualities" of human expression, action, accomplishment, failure, and aspiration. The ideal has two parts. One is to capture those qualities in the moment of metamorphosis, as the perceiver and perceived fuse. The other is to render them justly. The philosopher and novelist Iris Murdoch (1970) sheds light on this dual challenge. In her attempt to describe what it means to be moral, she draws on the poet Rainer Maria Rilke's letters about Cezanne. She writes: "Rilke said of Cezanne that he did not paint 'I like it', he painted 'There it is'. This is not easy, and requires, in art or morals, a discipline" (p. 59). "The greatest art is 'impersonal'," she goes on to write, "because it shows us the world, our world and not another, with a clarity which startles and delights us simply because we are not used to looking at the real world at all" (p. 65).

Murdoch's claim discloses a second level of meaning in Elkins's distinction between seeing as metamorphosis and as mechanism. In one sense, as mentioned at the start of this essay, the difference boils down to distinguishing biological operations of the eye from culturally and linguistically informed perception. However, at another level these acquired ways of perceiving can themselves become mechanical, with potentially deadening consequences. All too often, it seems, people look, judge, and move on—and seldom look again. Their seeing is flattening rather than responsive. I see a teacher standing by her door urging students to come in, sit down, and get organized, and I may see a busybody or somebody who enjoys power. However, if I'm willing to look again, I may discover that the teacher so values her students and their learning that she does not have a moment to lose. In the first instance, my seeing is mechanical, an unreflective result of a whole jumble of presuppositions I hold about teachers, schools, and classrooms. In the second instance, I'm moving beyond the "I like it or dislike it" stance that Rilke criticizes to one guided by a question such as "What is this?"

Murdoch seeks to highlight the genuine difficulty in learning to see what is there, rather than merely seeing what we expect or want to see. That difficulty finds expression in Cezanne's language of becoming the passing minute, being the sensitive plate, rendering oneself (metamorphosing) into an instrument capable of catching the world in its passing form. When that transformation happens, as it does in Cezanne's oeuvre, both truth and justice are served: truth because he has offered us insight into the world and our experience of it, and justice because, metaphorically speaking, he has let the world speak to us rather than merely submitting it to our will, desire, or fantasy. He has not pinned the world to a wall with an a priori, fixed frame of reference (or, put differently, he has not presumed the latter is the only way to look). Rather than binding perception before it has even had a chance to try itself out, he liberates it to engage a more fundamental source of obligation, namely, recognizing that the reality of the world always exceeds the terms of any framework or compound of theories.

Cezanne also expresses the idea of a dialogue or transaction. In poetic terms, in order to listen to the world one also has to speak to it. Holderlin calls out to the friendly gods, rather than passively awaiting their word. Cezanne, not the world, puts brush to canvas. He does so again and again. He shows his work to others. He writes about it. He lives it. In so doing, he acts as if the world needs his art as much as he needs it. Rilke thought poetry a mode of speaking that not only helps us to see the world in its reality, but that the world needs to sustain itself, especially now that humanity has gained the technological wherewithal to treat it as a mere thing rather than as a home. In his "Ninth Duino Elegy," Rilke (1923/1989) writes:

> *Here* is the time for the *sayable, here* is its homeland.
> Speak and bear witness. More than ever
> the Things that we might experience are vanishing, for
> what crowds them out and replaces them is an imageless act.
> An act under a shell, which easily cracks open as soon as
> the business inside outgrows it and seeks new limits.
> Between the hammers our heart
> endures, just as the tongue does
> between the teeth and, despite that,
> still is able to praise. (p. 201; emphasis in original)

For Rilke, to praise is to name, just as Holderlin as poet learned to name his teachers and his gratitude. It is not just names, however, but the impulse behind the naming that counts. The "sayable" encompasses everything we have named—in a previous line, Rilke mentions "house, bridge, fountain, gate, pitcher, fruit-tree, window"—and yet infused with a spirit of response rather than an ambition to grasp. Rilke's glance is not backwards, nor is he a Luddite. He implies that we should go on building homes and bridges and vehicles and all the rest. But there is a way to do so with the moral purpose of treating the world as a home rather than as a supermarket. We can treat the world as an existential partner that "calls to us" and makes a claim upon us, just as we make claims upon it. When Rilke writes that "here" (rather than "now") is the time for the sayable, he means in his very poem itself, and he means in all art and in all that might be artful in human life, which potentially encompasses the entirety of our makings and doings. Here is the time for the sayable. Gates, windows, fruit-trees—all of it—can become "Things" to praise rather than merely items to consume. We praise them when we attend to them, respect them, and see them within a totality of meaning. The capitalized T symbolizes Rilke's image of a wholly realized life of dwelling in the world, a life in which humans and world sojourn together rather than in alienation from each other. The passing minute of the world's life becomes not fleeting but full.

The diarist Etty Hillesum, a deep admirer of Rilke's poetry, draws from his work an image of guardianship, as if the world needs us humans to preserve its meanings and sustain its possibilities. Here is an entry from the last year of her life (cut short at all too young an age during World War II):

> I want to carry you in me, nameless, and pass you on with a new and tender gesture I did not know before. . . . I often used to think to myself as I walked about in Westerbork among the noisily bickering, all too energetic members of the Jewish Council: if only I could enter a small piece of their soul. If only I could be the receptacle of their better nature, which is sure to be present in all of them. Let me be rather than do. Let me be the soul in that body. And I would now and then discover in each one of them a gesture or a glance that took them out of themselves and of which they seemed barely aware. And I felt I was the guardian of that gesture or glance. (Hillesum, 1981/1996, p. 202)

Hillesum's acute perceptiveness positions her to discern the humanity in her harried, hard-pressed, and overworked colleagues. Her guardianship of that humanity, in the "nameless" gesture she creates in prose, issues from the moral responsiveness to her world that she has learned to cultivate.

Research articles are not diary entries, just as they are not paintings or poems. It would be a genuine loss of light, clarity, and instrumentality to conflate them. However, at least in some of its modes qualitative research on teaching surely demands that the inquirer become a guardian of gesture and glance, not out of a romantic urge to preserve the unpreservable, nor a hagiographic impulse to gush, but rather out of a commitment to render educational significances. This act can, in turn, influence others to remember to look and to attend.

Not everything in education needs fixing. Sometimes it's the perceiver's lens that most needs repair.

SEEING WITH

Gods, minutes, and gestures. Things, guardians, and gratitude. Holderlin, Cezanne, Rilke, and Hillesum share a solidarity with the unfathomable experience of living, and they share a desire to understand. One might say that they learned not so much to look *at* the world as to see *with* it, in a manner that Maurice Merleau-Ponty (1964) captures in describing some famous 20,000-year-old cave paintings in southern France:

> The animals painted on the walls of Lascaux are not there in the same way as the fissures and limestone formations. But they are not *elsewhere*. Pushed

forward here, held back there, held up by the wall's mass they use so adroitly, they spread around the wall without ever breaking from their elusive moorings in it. I would be at great pains to say *where* is the painting I am looking at. For I do not look at it as I do at a thing; I do not fix it in its place. . . . It is more accurate to say that I see according to it, or with it, than that I *see it.* (p. 164; emphasis in original)

Seeing is metamorphosis, not mechanism. Merleau-Ponty tries to formulate his sense that he is not a spectator of the world but rather is a participant in it. He is not a camera; he is a person. He can look "at" fissures and limestone formations and call it a day—although even at that level his seeing has already been transformed, as the very terms "fissure," "limestone," and "formation" imply (and a geologist might be gripped emotionally by those Things). As Merleau-Ponty notes, the animals spread across the walls. They move, undulate, and radiate. As he pays attention to them, they draw him in, and in a more than metaphorical sense. In technical terms, if he refused to give himself over to them, he would not see them in their ontological fullness. The animals would instead be there "in the same way" as the rock and cracks upon which they are painted. Merleau-Ponty would leave the cave the same person he was when he entered. Seeing can remain mechanism.

Where are the moral dimensions of teaching? Are they in the eye of the beholder? Or are they there in the classroom, "spread around" and over and in the actions of teachers and students? If they are there to be seen, how does one learn to see them? That question resided at the heart of The Moral Life of Schools Project, and it was Philip Jackson who made it possible for me to engage it. His Socratic presence set a daily example of what it means to believe in the worthiness of inquiry and to trust that one can learn to learn. His mode of inquiry suggested to me that giving free rein to human sympathies, disciplined through a crucible of hard work, can help one come to see the classroom world *with* the moral, just as Merleau-Ponty learned to look *with* the paintings on the walls at Lascaux. I remember vividly what it felt like to see the moral life of a classroom move, undulate, and radiate. I could not write things down fast enough.

Philip Jackson and the Nuances of Imagination

Maxine Greene

M Y INTEREST in Philip Jackson's multifaceted life work began with my reading of *Life in Classrooms* (1968). The book made me aware of particularities in the worlds of schooling I had never thought of before. Moreover, it made me realize something of what can happen to children when they become first graders or fifth graders rather than individual Jacks and Jills. I found the same sensitivity to the lives of young people in his studies of high schools and in *The Practice of Teaching* (1986). That book and his understanding of the qualitative aspects of teaching and learning expanded my concepts of what educational research could be. There did not have to be what I had thought of as a necessary either/or where the quantitative and the qualitative were concerned. Quantitative studies could be conducted without treating their subjects as cyphers; qualitative inquiries could be as rigorous and precise when exploring the lived experiences of distinctive human beings.

There was a memorable moment some years ago when I was chairing the Lecture Committee of the John Dewey Society and invited Philip Jackson to give the Dewey Lecture for that year. Obviously, we were delighted when he accepted and said his topic would be the work of William James. The day arrived and so did the lecturer, but without the expected manuscript under his arm. He mounted the platform, there was a hush, and suddenly he was William James. I do not know if I imagined the brocade vest or the flushed cheeks, nor if Philip really transformed himself into a kind of flimflam radical empiricist. I do know I felt James's presence on that hotel stage. Only much later did I find out that our lecturer had had theatrical experience as a child and that, at the time he performed for us, he was part of a group studying performance. I realized then that he had indeed been teaching when he played William James. A transient moment but a significant one for those of us who chose to pay heed.

I sat on a number of panels with Philip at conferences over the years, each time on the edge of my seat for fear of falling into sentimentality or being blown away by an ideological wind. Like other friends and colleagues, I cannot but hold in mind his pointed rebuttals, his demands for clarity, his unalloyed good sense. His turn to scholarship for its own sake (unusual for an educational theorist and practitioner) has led him into intense engagements with the writings of Kant, Hegel, and Dewey and probably several more. Involved as I have been with aesthetics and the several arts, I have found his critical study of Dewey's aesthetics to be particularly meaningful. Our shared enthusiasm for Wallace Stevens has moved me to reach more and more deeply into Stevens's poetry, and that has made me confront a variety of new questions regarding the relation between imagination and what is called "reality." They are questions of moment at this time in history, and Dr. Jackson has done much to help us distinguish between mere fancy or "building castles in the air" and authentic acts of imagination.

Teachers today cannot ignore the impact of fabricated media images on children and young adults. Given the ubiquity of these images—on cartoons, commercials, horror shows, and all sorts of situation comedies—it has become more and more difficult to tell the difference between the passive absorption of what is on the screen and the activities of imagination. Dewey wrote: "When old and familiar things are made new in experience, there is imagination. . . . There is always some measure of adventure in the meeting of mind and the universe, and this adventure is, in its measure, imagination" (LW.10.271, 272). Part of this adventure is the ability to summon up alternative realities—what might be, what could be. Attending to the play of young children, watching them pretend, we may find the origins of the capacity to look at things as if they were otherwise. To distract from such experience under the spell of more sensational imagery devised for the sake of advertising or persuasion is to leave the young vulnerable to mystifying and (too often) manipulative messages or information. Moreover, it is to leave even adolescents in confusion with regard to what is "news" and what is "fiction." Jackson's familiarity with the development of diverse children and his experiences as head of the Laboratory School in Chicago must have made him increasingly aware of the impact of reality shows and rendered more and more problematic the popular grasp of what can be depended on as real and what can only be fabrication.

All this has made me more and more interested in the concept of imagination and its ambiguities. I have no empirical evidence to demonstrate the ways in which imagination breaks through the limits of the given and reaches beyond what is thought to be the factual. Nor do I have evidence to explain how we suspend disbelief and enter into created worlds. How do such entries give us new perspectives, new understandings? It may help to look at changing approaches to the work of imagination. Certain ones clarify encounters with the "as if." Others shed light on human beings' persistent quest for final answers and epiphanies, for all their recognition that few such quests succeed.

The conclusion of the chapter called "Cetology" in Herman Melville's (1851/1981) *Moby Dick* suggests that no search for finality, no search for a completed system can ever or should ever succeed, whether the system has to do with the classification of whales or sailors or island men or metaphysical ideas:

> It was stated at the outset that this system would not be here and at once perfected. You cannot but plainly see that I have kept my word. But I now leave my cetological System standing thus unfinished even as the great Cathedral of Cologne was left, with the crane still standing upon the top of the uncompleted tower. For small erections may be finished by their first architects: grand ones, true ones, ever leave the copestone to posterity. God keep me from ever completing anything. This whole book is but a draught—nay, a draught of a draught. (p. 148)

If possibilities are fully realized, they are closed. If students shut their books on the assumption they have learned all there is to know, their education has ended.

Jackson's interest in children and young people, and his concern for the moral life and the ways in which different children survive in dark times, has led to an array of open questions. Rejecting fixities, turning away from relativism, few of us can avoid the problem of the relation between mind and reality; and, as educators, we are bound to confront the matter of the mind's role in constructing or constituting reality. Some of us cannot but be aware that debates about curricula and modes of teaching today arise out of ongoing philosophical conversations having to do with understanding, representation, and the pursuit of meaning. Jackson's (1986) contrast between what he calls "mimetic" and "transformative" education raises echoes from the history of ideas. The "mimetic" focuses on subject matter derived from the cumulative knowledge of the culture, its traditions, its sustaining values. The "transformative" emphasizes the use students make of such subject matter:

the critical-creative and interpretive thinking required for learning. Long recognized for his rejection of dualisms, Jackson has secured a visible position
in the pragmatic and experiential traditions. He has consistently avoided dichotomies in his proposals for pedagogical change. Concerned with synthesis, he has presented far more promising alternatives than those offered by
contesting curricular proponents—those arguing for the affective versus the
cognitive, for instance, or for the experiential versus imposed traditions and
skills.

His work is evocative of Immanuel Kant's inquiries into the nature of
knowledge and the signal role of imagination. For Kant, it was imagination
that was the fundamental condition of knowledge, and it was imagination that
effected the synthesis of cognition and sensation or sensory experience. Sensation provided the content of cognition, but sensation without cognition was
blind. Cognition without sensation was empty, purely abstract; but, being the
rational faculty, it shaped and ordered the otherwise formless material of
phenomenal appearances. Kant wrote, for instance, that the very existence
of nature depended on the exercise of cognition in introducing order and
regularity into what would otherwise be a chaos of sensations (Heidegger,
1929/1962, pp. 144–148). The importance of the imagination in synthesizing in this fashion appears in works of other philosophers as well. On occasion, their effort was to make a case for works of art as creating integrated
wholes removed from commonsense reality. Many, like the poets, were putting their stress on inner voices, on a recently discovered subjectivity.

All of this might be considered within a context of seismic social and
cultural changes. On the one side, great energies were being released; on the
other, increasing feelings of powerlessness, of invisible forces over which
there was no control. Some became aware of what would one day be called
"cultures of silence," numerous human beings, men and women, unable to
find words for telling their stories. In one of Wallace Stevens's poems, he spoke
of a language that he once heard as "the gibberish of the vulgate" but that
might become "a peculiar speech" he would try to use (Stevens, 1942/1982b,
p. 396). "To compound imagination's Latin with the lingua franca" (p. 396)
might mean enriching the language of the arts and perhaps closing the gap
existing between the very poor and lost and artists who might speak for them.
We need only think of farmers forced off their farms and villages into the
cities and the burgeoning factories. We need only think of the peculiar experience of becoming part of a crowd for the first time, anonymous among
strangers. Blake, Baudelaire, Kierkegaard, Emerson, Thoreau, Hawthorne,
Wordsworth—each in his own way—worked to capture and find words for
what was happening as the "machine" crashed into the "garden," as cities grew
and individuals were asked to redefine themselves as citizens, members of a
"public." This required acts of the imagination, if only for the sake of experi-

encing a degree of empathy for persons they did not know. Then there was the need to impart an objective reality to the concept of human rights. As Dewey was to say years later, "human rights" was an invention required to combat another invention called "the divine right of kings." Both were imaginative constructs, one bringing together a notion of natural law and a human endowment; the other, relating that endowment to the work of God.

The images of "Kublai Khan" or "The Ancient Mariner," invented by Samuel Taylor Coleridge, not only bring the exotic and the remote into the consciousness of the reader. They activate powers akin to those that allow us to treat the idea of rights as if rights were objectively real. It seems almost contradictory to say that Coleridge, writing about imagination in his *Bibliographia Literaria*, excluded the notion of the mimetic and put his stress on imagination's productive or creative capacities. They were what made possible the "exemplastic" relation among diverse and often opposing ideas, qualities, feelings, and images.

Our recollection of certain metaphors (the moon as a "ghostly galleon," "Dr. Eckleburg's eyes" on a billboard as God's eyes looking at the "valley of dust") may make clear what that "exemplastic" relation can mean. For Coleridge, there were a primary and secondary imagination also to be taken into account. The primary imagination was "the living power and prime agent of human perception" (quoted in Warnock, 1978, p. 92). The secondary imagination "dissolves, diffuses, dissipates in order to create" (p. 92).

The secondary imagination, then, played with and sometimes overturned timeworn structures. It brought together discordant qualities and fragments into new structures, new designs. Doing so, it defamiliarized familiar objects, made them seem strange and new. There were those who relished the new vistas, the new profiles made available to them. There were others who pined for a lost coherence, who listened for echoes of old tunes. Still others picked up the threads of family stories or folktales, made storytelling quilts. Imagination can reach in more than one direction after all: It can reweave the fabrics of memory and, even as it explores and reinvents the past, it can weave fabrics that appear to suggest wholly new orders of things.

Seeking clues in diaries, personal narratives, and correspondence, we can detect tides of desolation and tides of stubborn hope and optimism. We realize that people read in different ways and on different levels. We realize as well how much depends on schooling, on education in church and family. Allowing for the multiplicity of interpretations and responses, we can still imagine something of the temper of the times. We can conjoin the colors, shapes, and imagery in paintings of the moment with poetry, the liturgies of the moment with music and ceremonies in the community. We can feel the ambivalences, the oversimplifications; we can sense the doubleness in personalities, the affirmations and the denials.

As always in times of sweeping and uneven change, many felt a shaking of the foundations. We might think of Melville's Captain Vere on the heaving deck of the ship called *The Indomitable* in the story *Billy Budd*. The captain has to choose between complying with the law of the sea and being true to his personal conviction, to his emotional certainty, and indeed to the feelings of the crew and their attachment to "Baby Budd." He decides, of course, in accord with principles that Billy must be hung from the yardarm of the ship for having socked the dreaded character Claggart with a blow that turned out to be fatal, however unintentional that outcome was on Billy's part. There was no universally acknowledged authority on ship or shore, no final definition of right and wrong, no anchorage in sight.

There were, now and then, imagined images like Shelley's skylark, still a symbol of freedom, still a symbol of flight toward possibility. But there was also the strangeness of John Keats's poem "Ode on a Grecian Urn," an enactment of fever and chill by a dying poet. The poet's voice is addressing the classical urn with its engraved figures, its funeral procession, the rhythm of dancing and death. He ends, perhaps sardonically, perhaps desperately, "Beauty is truth, truth beauty—that is all / Ye know on earth, and all ye need to know." Can this ever be all we "know"? And does he, or anyone (alive or dead) have the right to tell us that something is all we know or need to know?

For many there was a feeling of emptiness, a void. Seeking reassurance, some rediscovered evangelical faiths. There were times (in 1830, in 1848, in 1870) when passing "revolutions," with differing faces on the front lines and in the parliaments, stamped their bourgeois or *sans culottes* or radical extremist views on the faces of the aimless flaneurs like Flaubert's Frederic Moreau in *A Sentimental Education*. Too many people, perhaps like Emma Bovary, lived hallucinatory lives, giving way to the lures of consumerism, romance, adultery, and unattainable urban luxuries. As in our own time, ordinary people were stirred to quixotic imaginings. Yes, there were utopian dreams and dystopian dreams. Those drawn to the works of Marx and Engels spoke of determinisms, of an inexorable dialectic, of a good and equal society to be won by a proletarian revolution—in time, in time. It was difficult to speak of the possible in the face of the determined, but it was necessary in the shadow of visions like those to be described in *Brave New World*, *Walden Two*, *A Clockwork Orange*, or *1984*. Anything is possible where imagination is concerned, when it is freed from its mainly synthesizing role. But if it is tamed or shamed in its spontaneous expressions, the process of humanization itself is thwarted.

To speak of William Wordsworth here is not to introduce a prophetic voice. Yes, he is canonical—a White, middle-class intellectual, male but opened to the female consciousness through his attachment to his sister Dorothy. Unlike many of his contemporaries, he turned the "visionary power" that was imagination not only on what he "recollected in tranquility," not only on "the growth of a poet's mind," but on what might be, what could be, what was not yet. Having been passionately committed to the ideals of the French Revolution, he fell into despair at its collapse. First, he took refuge in the study of mathematics; then he tried to immerse himself in the throbbing life of London. Like Kierkegaard and Baudelaire, for instance, he suffered the pressures and anonymity of the crowd. Unlike others, he had a childhood in the Lake Country to fall back on; and, against that background, he felt afflicted by the artifices and the constraints of city life, walled in somehow; and he knew he needed to return. Lakes, mountains, wildflower fields, rural cottages, aged and familiar faces: He made them live in "The Prelude," made them the stuff of his imagining. Doing so, he was able to retrieve images of himself as a child rowing, climbing in search of a robin's nest, hanging off a crag with ghostly winds blowing, giving him "an obscure sense of possible sublimity" (quoted in Warnock, 1978, p. 203).

The "sublime," for many, referred to vast landscapes reaching into the distances, to overwhelming mountains, the dark depths of gorges, the icy peaks that seemed to scrape the sky. Experiencing such scenes, people felt something unreachable, occasioning breathlessness, moving them beyond speech. What they saw was not beneficent or heavenly in any sense. But it drew many beyond the flatlands of daily life; it pulled them toward horizons never seen before. Wordsworth, writing of a "possible sublimity," said later that, no matter how people mature, no matter how much they learn, "there is still something to pursue" (quoted in Warnock, 1978, p. 203). This notion, for me, conjoins imagination not only to the idea of untapped possibility but also to the idea of learning as ongoing—to paraphrase Melville, not just a draft but the draft of a draft. And I would hope that our learners, each in his or her own language, would say with him, "Dear God, keep me from ever completing anything."

For Emily Dickinson, "The Possible's slow fuse is lit by the Imagination" (Dickinson, 1891/1960, p. 689). Even to say "slow fuse" is to indicate something other than a sudden burst of insight. "Possible" may begin to imply "feasible," something to be attained by deliberate action. To echo Paul Ricoeur, imagination is a passion for the possible. This notion is quite different from Kant's idea that imagination not only underlies but synthesizes cognition and sensation; but, at the same time, it suggests that the very notion of going beyond what is known to the unpredictable, to what might be, becomes a legitimate epistemological concern. When John Dewey spoke of the ways in which we think, he was likely to emphasize the importance of rehearsing in imagination what might follow from a particular line of inquiry. For him, this move demanded a willingness to reach beyond mere facts to imagining intellectual possibility.

For Dewey and for Jackson, the self does not preexist the choices we make and the actions we take. The self is created by choice and action. For there to be reflective choosing, there has to be a consideration of alternative courses of action, a process that clearly involves acts of imagination. Consequences must be imagined if we are to make intelligent decisions; and those consequences must be viewed in the contexts of a social situation, personal predilection, and cumulative meanings. Very often, as Jean-Paul Sartre has suggested, it is from the vantage point of what might be that we are moved to act. What he called social vision might arouse people from passivity to discover what is lacking in the existing situation: health plans, pension plans for working people, the right of graduate students to join unions, the protection of free speech in classrooms, and equity when it comes to admissions.

We might think in terms of beginnings, of spaces opening before us. They are the spaces of possibility where we can achieve our freedom, in part by taking note of what is lacking in the spaces of which we are aware, of the deficiencies, of what calls out for repair. This is the domain of the social imagination, turning attention to what ought to be, what might be on the Gulf Coast, in Darfur, in schools marked for their "savage inequality," in places where minorities are persecuted, on the media where the news is falsified. At the moment, there is a widespread interest in "social justice" curricula and in teaching about social justice at all levels in the school. Not only do the terms need to be clarified; the character of the just society must be imagined and defined. What is possible, what is feasible for students of different ages to pursue? Can social justice be achieved within the political and economic system that presently exists? Can we ever expect a total resolution of the conflicts, the problems on all sides? Might not the best we can do be "a draft of a draft" if only we continue the pursuit? It is no longer the "sublime" or the equation of Truth and Beauty. It is the life-giving incompleteness of being on the way, of never being sure if we can find the road that "might make all the difference." We cannot exhaust the nuances of imagination if we do not include the moral imagination—which involves most centrally our relations to the Other, whoever that Other may be. It may be, first of all, the nurture of a capacity to see through the eyes of another, on occasion to feel with the other. It may require acts of empathy, which itself demands acts of imagination. Novels and plays, because they have to do with the transactions of human beings who have somehow been rendered transparent by an artist with their ambivalences, their flaws, their virtues made approximately clear—and always much left in the dark. What is important is the willingness to accept our ethical responsibility and become willing to come face to face with the particularity of the woman in Darfur, the homeless person in the shelter, the child shorn of his uniqueness, and the significance of choosing ourselves as teachers with all the imagination and commitment now required.

I conclude inconclusively with lines from Wallace Stevens's "The Man with the Blue Guitar" (Stevens, 1937/1982a, p. 179) and in homage to Philip Jackson:

> The world washed in his imagination,
> The world was a shore, whether sound or form
>
> Or light, the relic of farewells,
> Rock, of valedictory echoings,
>
> To which his imagination returned,
> From which it sped, a bar in space,
>
> Sand heaped in the clouds, giant that fought
> Against the murderous alphabet:
>
> The swarm of thoughts, the swarm of dreams
> Of inaccessible Utopia.
>
> A mountainous music always seemed
> To be falling and to be passing away.

CHAPTER 5

Portrait of a Thinker

Robert Boostrom

I FIRST met Philip Wesley Jackson in 1986. I was a prospective graduate student, and he asked me what I was interested in. I talked about something I called "intellectual closure"—that is, the tendency of all of us to rush to believe things, including many things that are simply wrong—and about how I had studied this phenomenon in high school students when I was a teacher back in Dallas, Texas. What my wife remembers about the meeting (she was there, too) is feeling immediately that this man would be very important in my life.

Within a couple of years I became one of Phil Jackson's research assistants and eventually a co-author on *The Moral Life of Schools* (Jackson, Boostrom, & Hansen, 1993), but events that occurred almost 20 years later testify even more tellingly to the keenness of my wife's insight about his importance in my life. I worked on a book about thinking (still pondering that topic I'd mentioned to Phil in 1986), and I never showed him one page of it until it was in print. I was so tied to his influence and support that I wanted to prove (at least to myself) that I could do it on my own.

Of course, traces of his influence and support haunt every page of the book. How could it be otherwise? I was writing about thinking, and Phil Jackson is my epitome of a thinker. He might just as well be sitting naked on a rock with his chin resting on the back of his hand.

But why do I say that about him? What is it about Philip Wesley Jackson that makes the eulogistic sense of "thinker" fit him so perfectly?

PUZZLEMENT AND THINKING

Part of what makes Phil Jackson a thinker is his genuine puzzlement. Has anyone else ever asked so many questions? Every time he tackles a topic, he begins with a question. The first essay in *The Practice of Teaching* (1986) opens like this:

> What must teachers know about teaching? What knowledge is essential to their work? Is there a lot to learn or just a little? Is it easy or difficult? How is such knowledge generated and confirmed? Indeed, dare we even call it knowledge in the strict sense of the term? Is not much of what guides the actions of teachers nothing more than opinion, not to say out-and-out guesswork? But even if that were so, what of the remainder? If *any* of what teachers claim to know about teaching qualifies as knowledge (and who dares deny that some does?), what can be said of its adequacy? How complete is it? Does much remain to be discovered or do the best of today's teachers already know most of what there is to learn? And whether the bulk of it is fully known or yet to be discovered, what, if anything, must be added to such knowledge to ready the teacher for his or her work? In other words, is there more to teaching than the skilled application of something called know-how? If so, what might that be? (p. 1; emphasis in original)

In *John Dewey and the Philosopher's Task* (2002b), he begins by puzzling about what went on in Dewey's mind:

> Why, I wondered, did Dewey find the task of introducing *Experience and Nature* sufficiently challenging to take it up on four separate occasions? More important, why was he dissatisfied, or seemingly so, with each successive attempt? (p. xvii)

In *Untaught Lessons* (1992b), he begins by puzzling about his own life story:

> What was Mrs. Henzi's role in contributing to my initial success and in nurturing my desire for more math? What else, beyond rules of algebra, did I learn under her tutelage? (p. 4)

Later, in a different essay from the same book, he reflects on a poem by Galway Kinnell and introduces the "question that will come to dominate" his analysis:

> Why should a grown man revisit the school of his childhood? . . . What are the plaguing thoughts that might propel someone on such a journey? . . . How can the past continue to be illuminating? What can it reveal that is not already within the ken of our vision? (pp. 24–25)

And later still, in the final essay from the same book, he puzzles about some conclusions he comes to:

> Let me restate the problem as it now stands. I am convinced that teaching has made a difference, a big difference in my life and at the same time I am uncertain, very uncertain, about what that difference consists of. Does that make sense? Can those two conditions coexist? (p. 77)

All of this questioning could be seen as a rhetorical device—a way of getting readers involved in the topic or of sharpening the exposition and moving it forward. The questions certainly serve those purposes.

But the questions Jackson asks seem real to me. What I mean by this is that often something that sounds like a question isn't really a question at all. This can occur when an answer is presumed to be obvious. If someone asks, "Should we do something about schools that aren't performing?" the answer is supposed to be yes. It isn't a real question. Another sort of ersatz question occurs when an answer is irrelevant. Talking about the operation of major league baseball teams, a National League executive asked, "Why would new owners want to come into a city and create the perception they're tearing up their club?" (Stark, 2006). It sounds like a question, but it doesn't call for an answer. The speaker is making a statement (owners wouldn't do this) in the form of a question.

Jackson's questions are different. They open new doors of possibilities. They sound like the musings of someone who is seeking answers but is not at all certain what those answers are. And the lack of certainty that these questions suggest says something important about Phil Jackson as a thinker. Questions that issue from genuine puzzlement are essential to philosophy because certainty puts an end to thinking. This is the hazard posed by those "scientifically inclined philosophers" who

> tend to "deny, discount or pervert the obvious and immediate facts of gross experience" in favor of the facts provided by science. When that happens, Dewey concludes, "philosophy itself commits suicide." . . . All that remains is a filling in of the blanks through a dialectical process of ratiocination. That process may take some time to complete, true enough, but that it has a rational terminus remains uncontested, once the first brick of certainty has been tapped into place. (Jackson, 2002b, p. 10)

Ask pretend questions, and there is nothing to think about. Replace questions with facts, and philosophy dies. To think is to be puzzled and to question. In Phil Jackson's questions I see his thinking mind at work.

LIFE AND THINKING

Does Phil Jackson choose to be puzzled? Or is questioning an inborn trait, like brown eyes or size-9 feet? Or are questions thrust upon Jackson in some other way?

My sense of the man is that he sets out "to rake the leaves away," hoping even "to watch the water clear," but that each layer of leaves removed reveals a new layer. For instance, he confesses in *John Dewey and the Philosopher's Task* (2002b) that he is unwilling "to put too much stock" in his finding that Dewey moved away from the hard sciences and toward the humanities "because it comes too close to what I wanted to find. I belatedly must admit that from the start I covertly hoped to find Dewey edging away from the goals and ambitions of the hard sciences" (p. 98).

In other words, after "puzzling over the odd history of [Dewey's] repeated attempts to introduce *Experience and Nature*" (2002b, p. xvi) and arriving at what he felt was a sound interpretation of the direction of Dewey's mind, Jackson finds himself puzzling over the reliability of his judgment. Have I, he wonders, found only what I wanted to find? Have I, he might add (though he doesn't), been too influenced by my own history, by my own move from the "hard science" of educational psychology to philosophy and the arts?

I can imagine Phil Jackson, sitting in his study, staring at the computer screen, reading from his draft of *John Dewey and the Philosopher's Task*, asking himself if he believes what he's written. His reflections on Dewey's struggles with the nature of experience will sound to some like the most removed of intellectual abstractions—a move straight "into the fog"—but Jackson (2002b) embraces this move, just as he said Dewey embraced it and rejected the alternative:

> Moving away from the fog essentially means avoiding all human entanglements. It means turning one's back on the problems that beset the bulk of humanity. It means playing it safe academically, answering the standard questions and using the approved procedures for answering them. (p. 101)

In other words, heading "into the fog" means welcoming human entanglements and putting every idea to the test: What does this idea mean to me and to those I live with and love? How does this bear on my world and my life?

Life was an important word for Dewey, who used it "to denote the whole range of experience, individual and racial." When we talk about someone's life, he said, we aren't talking about physiology. We're talking about "an account of social antecedents; a description of early surroundings, of the conditions and occupation of the family; of the chief episodes in the development of character; of signal struggles and achievements; of the individual's hopes, tastes, joys, and sufferings" (MW.9.5).

This same attitude toward "life" is evident in Jackson's work. It's no coincidence that two of his books are called *Life in Classrooms* and *The Moral Life of Schools*. And this sensitivity to life helps to explain the origin of all those questions. When our deepest philosophical reflections, our purest abstractions, are rooted in life, we cannot help asking the sorts of questions that Phil Jackson asks. From this perspective, every conclusion reached by philosophical reflection issues from experience and returns to experience. Questions arise out of life and return to life, because each conclusion is a matter of "doing something overtly to bring about the anticipated result" (Dewey, MW.9.157), so that each conclusion is a new starting point.

Here is an example of what I mean. It comes from *John Dewey and the Philosopher's Task* (2002b):

> Why does [Dewey] seem drawn to the image of the philosopher as either a mapmaker or a sea traveler? Can one envision just any philosopher of Dewey's day—Bertrand Russell, let's say, or Carnap or Whitehead—making use of either of those images? (p. 58)

It would be easy for a reader to pass over Dewey's characterization of the philosopher as mapmaker or sea traveler and to think of nothing more than a vague impression of a map or of someone on the deck of a ship. Perhaps even likelier is the reader who treats the image as a proposition: P = M or ST. M possesses certain characteristics (draws outlines, sketches terrain, shows routes), and P figuratively possesses those same characteristics.

But Phil Jackson gets inside Dewey's image. It's as if he can see and hear Dewey talking about the task of philosophy. The second question he asks— "Can one envision just any philosopher of Dewey's day . . . ?"—is admittedly not a real question; it's one of those statements masquerading as a real question, because it's clear that Jackson is stating that he emphatically cannot imagine Russell or Carnap or Whitehead talking about philosophy this way. But this statement heightens the puzzle of the first question. Why does Dewey talk this way about philosophy? What does Dewey mean? And what is it that makes Dewey so different from his philosophical peers?

These questions arise because, for Phil Jackson, "Dewey" is not a label attached to some propositions; it's the name of a friend, someone who lived a life. Phil is curious about what makes his friend philosophize the way he does. Phil has much to say about his friend, including the complaint that his friend is not as forthright as he might be about "the difficulties that he himself experienced as a philosopher" (2002b, p. 99). Perhaps this is why Phil shares his own difficulties and uncertainties. And once we begin to talk about "the chief episodes in the development of character; of signal struggles and achievements; of the individual's hopes, tastes, joys, and sufferings"(Dewey, MW.9.5)—once we embody philosophy in life and welcome human entanglements, the questions come unbidden. We realize that the quest for certainty is a false goal because it can only be satisfied "outside the boundary of human experience" (p. 101). Puzzlement—and the thinking it engenders—is part of the *human* condition.

CHANGE AND THINKING

So far I have said that Phil Jackson fits my image of a thinker because he asks questions—lots of them—and because his questions are rooted in life. Together, these two conditions—puzzlement and life—imply a third condition: the inevitability of change.

Openness to change is not always seen as an appropriate characteristic in a philosopher or anyone else. In a press conference held on October 4, 2005, President Bush (2005) spoke about his nominee for the Supreme Court, Harriet Miers. He said, "I don't want to put somebody on the bench who's this way today and changes. That's not what I'm interested in. I'm interested in finding somebody who shares my philosophy today and will have that same philosophy 20 years from now."

Some people probably share this attitude that one's philosophy—one's thinking—should remain frozen, but Phil Jackson is not one of those people. As in so many ways, here, too, his mode of mind parallels John Dewey's:

> One of the most endearing features of John Dewey's personality was his openness to ideas and suggestions whatever their source. At the very height of his philosophical career and even toward its very close, he was always sensitive to the possibility of new facets and dimensions of experience, to new problems and new aspects of old problems. (Sidney Hook, quoted in Jackson, 2002b, p. 24)

Phil Jackson's sensitivity to new facets and dimensions of experience appears both in the topics he takes up for reflection and in what he says about them. For example, in *Untaught Lessons* he reflects on his ninth-grade algebra teacher, a poem ("The Schoolhouse"), and classroom observations of a first-grade teacher—a rather ordinary list until we remember that from these subjects, he intends to learn something new about what teachers can and must know about teaching. That is, Phil Jackson honestly believes that his experiences as a high school freshman in algebra class can be revisited for insights into teaching. He honestly believes that by burrowing into these old memories, he will find new problems and new aspects of old problems. He believes he will be changed by remembering Mrs. Henzi and her algebra class.

Phil Jackson also honestly believes that if he attends to and thinks about a poem, it will change him; he will learn something new about teaching and learning. He believes in the power of the arts to open us to the world and freshen our insight.

Most surprising of all, Phil Jackson honestly believes that by sitting in a first-grade classroom he can learn about teaching—not just about one teacher's practice, but about the practice of teaching itself. He believes that if he sits in an ordinary classroom and pays attention closely enough and thinks about what he is seeing and hearing, it will be possible for him to "move from ordinary experience to the heights of abstraction" (2002b, p. 99).

In short, Phil Jackson believes that when we think, when we dig deeply into genuine questions that arise from everyday experience, we are likely to see everything—the problem, the world, and ourselves—differently. Thinking changes us, although to put it that way may be misleading. We don't think in order to change. We change because we think.

CHUTZPAH AND THINKING

The inevitability of change makes thinking unpredictable. We begin to think about an ordinary event—say, a first-grade teacher teaching a reading lesson—something so ordinary that everyone acts as if it is simple and perfectly understood. But as we think about it, we discover that it isn't so simple and that we don't understand it at all.

Maybe this is why one of Phil Jackson's favorite words is *hunch*. I say this on the basis of many hours of conversation with him, not after counting how many times the word appears in his writing. But it does appear, and when it does, it says something about the kind of thinker Phil Jackson is. Near the end of *John Dewey and the Philosopher's Task* (2002b), Jackson writes, "My hunch was that [Dewey's] apparent difficulty [introducing *Experience and Nature*] may have reflected some discomfort with his own view of philosophy" (p. 96).

Is this use of *hunch* academic hedging? Is it an acknowledgment of the unpredictability about where thinking will lead? Should I read it as an expression of humility?

Let's take a closer look at what Jackson is saying. Before he began his close analysis of Dewey's several introductions to *Experience and Nature*, he had a hunch, something on the order of a feeling, a guess, or a vague surmise. He sensed that Dewey felt "some discomfort with his own view of philosophy."

Now, what's interesting is how Phil chose to respond to this hunch. He might have said, "Hm, that's interesting," and then have moved on to a project based on something more promising than a hunch. He might have said, "Well, maybe it's true, but how many people care whether or not John Dewey was philosophically uncomfortable?" and then have moved on to a project with wider appeal. He might even have said, "Yes, I think it makes sense, but I doubt that I could ever prove it," and then have moved on to a project more likely to achieve an incontrovertible result. But what he did do was to throw himself into a prolonged study of Dewey's introductions—a study that would, in the end, merely tend to confirm his hunch. This is a response that seems to me to show intellectual nerve and self-confidence—in short, chutzpah.

I first saw this trait in Phil Jackson when we started to work on *The Moral Life of Schools* project. We launched the project, met with the teachers, and visited their classrooms "long before we had a firm idea of what we would actually be looking for when our work began or even of what terms like *moral* and *moral life* could possibly mean when they were applied to what goes on in schools" (Jackson et al., 1993, p. xv). So if we were ignorant of what "moral life" was or of what we would find out about it, on what was our project (involving 3 researchers and 18 teachers over a period of 3 years) based? A hunch:

> Our hunch that teachers and school administrators are only partially aware of how they contribute to the moral upbringing of their students led us to believe that there is much to be learned about the moral influence schools and teachers have on their students. (p. xv)

A thinker trusts hunches and acts on them. A thinker does not wait for projects that guarantee incontrovertible results or popular acclaim. A thinker goes where the hunches lead, and that requires intellectual chutzpah.

IMPRACTICALITY AND THINKING

The characteristics of a thinker that I have attributed to Phil Jackson—a tendency to be in a state of puzzlement, a habit of rooting intellectual questions in life, an openness to change, and intellectual self-confidence—often arouse in others a kind of dismissiveness that focuses on the thinker's impracticality. So common is this response that I offer it as the fifth marker of a thinker. Here is an example from a review of Jackson's book, *John Dewey and the Lessons of Art* (1998b):

> Despite my hopes for a more practical discussion of Dewey's conceptions of the lessons of art and their application to education, as implied in the book's title and the introduction's opening statement, this later statement in the intro-

duction reveals the more musing style of Jackson's writing and his modest intentions to "say something" as opposed to inspire action. Although his main focus
on how Dewey's theory of the transformative power of art can "modify irrevocably our habitual ways of thinking, feeling, and perceiving" (p. xiv), does not
seem modest at all, his intention is first to present Dewey's theory and then to
muse over its relevance for contemporary life and education. By the book's end,
it becomes apparent that the responsibility is on the reader to decide how art's
lessons might be applied concretely. (Costantino, 2001)

The reviewer seems dissatisfied by the lack of a "practical discussion"
precisely stating "how art's lessons might be applied concretely." She offers
Jackson's "musing style" as a marker of this shortcoming. Musing, it seems,
indicates to her a failure to get to the point. While aiming to "modify irrevocably our habitual ways of thinking, feeling, and perceiving" is hardly a "modest" intention (Costantino acknowledges), neither is it a practical one because
it does not "inspire action"—it does not tell readers what to do. Thinking—
even if it changes how we view the world—is (for Costantino) simply not
enough.

The complaint is familiar enough: Thinkers are dreamy people with their
head in the clouds, people who don't pay attention to the details of everyday
life, people who don't get things done.

One of the big problems with thinkers (according to those who are concerned with practical, concrete action) is that they ask the wrong sorts of
questions. Consider again some of Phil Jackson's questions:

- Is there more to teaching than the skilled application of something
  called know-how?
- Why, I wondered, did Dewey find the task of introducing *Experience
  and Nature* sufficiently challenging to take it up on four separate
  occasions?
- What else, beyond rules of algebra, did I learn under [Mrs. Henzi's]
  tutelage?
- How can the past continue to be illuminating? What can it reveal that
  is not already within the ken of our vision?
- I am convinced that teaching has made a difference, a big difference
  in my life and at the same time I am uncertain, very uncertain, about
  what that difference consists of. Does that make sense? Can those two
  conditions coexist?

Now, suppose that each of these questions were answered. How would
the answers change the world? What difference would they make?

Let's suppose that we know that there is more to teaching than the skilled
application of know-how, and further, that we even know what that some-

thing more is. We still have to decide what to do about it or how to do what needs to be done. It is still true that "the responsibility is on the reader to decide" how to act in light of this insight.

Let's suppose that we come to understand how the past can be illuminating and what it can reveal. Does this change how we teach history (or anything else)? Does this insight entail any particular action regarding curriculum, assessment, or school policy? Again, "the responsibility is on the reader to decide" how (or whether) the results of this sort of musing bear on the activity of everyday life.

In short, I have to say that Costantino is right. Phil Jackson is not much concerned with providing her with a recipe for teaching art class. Instead of prescribing action, he seeks to modify our "habitual ways of thinking, feeling, and perceiving." He writes as if he believes that this investigation into ourselves is the most important topic about which anyone can muse. He writes like someone whose words are living thoughts, rather than the pronouncements of cold conclusions. He writes like someone who believes that "to move from ordinary experience to the heights of abstraction" is a worthy endeavor, rather than (as Costantino suggests) a waste of time.

In a world dominated by "the bottom line," it is certain that any genuine thinker will be dismissed as impractical. When all human activities are reduced to an equation of outcome per input (say, a school test score divided by dollars spent per child), there will be little understanding (and even less appreciation) of those thinkers who treat life as if it is inexhaustibly enigmatic and constantly capable of yielding new insights to those who take the time to muse.

RAKING THE LEAVES AWAY

This portrait of Philip Wesley Jackson as thinker has dealt with my own idiosyncratic list of characteristics. I haven't said anything about the breadth of his knowledge, about his intellectual honesty, about the terms he's coined, or about the forms of inquiry he's inspired. And there are undoubtedly many other reasons that other people would find for calling Phil Jackson a thinker. But these seem to me a good starting point. He begins in puzzlement, he roots his questions in life, he revels in change, he follows his hunches with chutzpah, and he believes in the pragmatic value of thinking (but is seen by others as impractical). When I shape these elements into a portrait, what I see is a youthful spirit. Here is a curious child raking the leaves away from the surface of the spring, not as chore, but for the delight of finding out what lies beneath, emboldened by the hope of seeing something never seen before.

CHAPTER 6

Jackson's Pedagogy for Existential Learning

René V. Arcilla

IMAGINE YOU are the apprentice of a master craftsman. After many years of hard work and setbacks, you manage at last to produce something satisfying his scrutiny, say, a glass bead game. Having thus attuned yourself to the demands of the craft, you confidently venture forth to ply your trade—only to be greeted by general perplexity, even derision. "Who needs these games? Don't you know we're in the middle of an educational crisis around here!"

It has been over 20 years since I was a student of Philip Jackson's. That apprenticeship changed my life. Glass-bead-game making, that is to say, philosophy of education, is my calling, although its marginality has indeed given me pause. Actually, that is an understatement: I have rarely gone too long before being reminded, once again, that hardly anyone has the faintest idea of the point of this work. And then I have to confront the fact that I am not sure of it either.

How ironical it is that I learned philosophy of education from a philosopher of education who never communicated to his circle the philosophy of his education. Of course, the problem may be simply that I was too dense; however, after many conversations with other Jackson acolytes, it is pretty clear that I am in crowded company. Nevertheless, what I want to try to explain in this essay is why I find this irony—seriously—truly marvelous. Part of my motivation, I have to admit, is an irrepressible impulse to crow that I have finally solved the homework assignment, just in time for the teacher's post-retirement Festschrift. Mainly, however, I would like to offer my own students and colleagues the beginnings of some reasons that philosophy of education, or at least a certain pedagogical approach to it, is a vital exercise of our very being. But, I hasten to emphasize, faithful to the master's teaching, only the beginnings.

So what exactly is this approach? It starts, as I remember, with students from all the various programs in Chicago's Department of Education, and a few from other parts of the university as well, filing into Judd 110. Math MAT candidates, a few liberal arts undergraduates, doctoral students in quantitative methods, early childhood development, sociology of education, and more, in addition to the handful of would-be philosophers of education: What are we all doing in the same room? The official answer is that Philosophy of Education is a required course for all education majors. But why? Whatever the reason, when Jackson arrives attention turns to him, and to our books. Dewey's *Democracy and Education* makes some sense as a text to study, however outdated, but Plato's *Meno*, or the *Nicomachean Ethics*? Furthermore, if you were hooked by this class and found yourself inclined to take other Jackson courses, the choices had titles like Wittgenstein as Educator, Emerson as Educator, Coleridge as Educator. You started to get the distinct sense that had he the interest, he could just as plausibly offer courses on Lucretius, Emily Dickinson, or Ozu Yasujiro, other "educators" who scarcely speak of education. In any case, class begins, and soon we find ourselves mulling over in conversation—in these years, Jackson never lectured—the meaning of, for instance, the line in *Emile*, "everything degenerates in the hands of man." At some point, inevitably, one of us, a touch impatiently, rises to say something like: "So Rousseau is claiming that we need a natural education. But even if that made sense in response to problems in the ancien régime, why should we, and how could we, actually offer such an education on the South Side of Chicago?" Amazingly, Jackson always managed to steer such questions toward others closer to, "How can we make sense of the apparent discrepancy, then, between how Rousseau uses the term *nature* on page 205 and what he says on page 415?" More often than not, after people have weighed in from all corners of the room in conflicting ways, class ends with us more puzzled than ever.

I am suggesting that there is more that is perplexing about this approach to teaching philosophy of education than the complexities of its texts. I would break it down into three or four questions: Why are we, present and future educational specialists, gathered together in the first place? Why are we summoned to study these kinds of humanistic and artistic texts, ones that stem from an entirely different time, place, and set of circumstances and that concern themselves with education only implicitly or secondarily? And why do we focus less on determining the practical value of their visions of the world and education and more on mere exegesis of what those visions are? Occasionally, one or another of us would work up the nerve to address these misgivings to Jackson, but to my recollection, he always let them glance off of him and declined to reply directly and at length. Is it that there are no satisfactory answers, and if so, what does that say about the real value of his classes? The meaning of this silence constitutes still another troubling question. Let me see if I can address them in some kind of order.

Why were we there? Again, what motivates this question is that our future roles as diverse educational experts would appear to call at that point for specialized instruction and training, not for some kind of common learning experience. The latter belongs in a collegiate liberal arts curriculum. In graduate professional school, the last stop before real work, knowledge should be directly tied to use, and obviously what is useful for a lawyer is not going to be so for a physician, what helps the kindergarten teacher will do nothing for the educational psychologist.

For the moment, I will not quarrel with this common wisdom, but I do want to set it aside and return to it later. Instead of asking the question rhetorically, let me press it in a different way. Radicalizing our doubt about why we should be there, in that room, rather than somewhere else more relevant to our vocational interests, imagine wondering why we were there rather than nowhere at all. We can each conceive of any number of alternative lives for us that do not include Philosophy of Education class. Add to these one more, not exactly for us but concerning us: that we are not even alive, that we do not exist. Why, then, do we exist? In explanation, we can reconstruct a chain of events that caused our birth and sustained us; conversely, we can again conceive of alternative histories that never got around to producing us. Now let us, by analogy with the above exercise regarding our existence, consider one more alternative to these histories: that none of them, indeed nothing at all, exists. If this is at least conceivable as a possibility, then we may ask: Why does anything exist rather than nothing at all? Is existence, at bottom, utterly contingent, or is there some kind of reason for it? Why are we, or anything, there (Nagel, 2004; Rundle, 2004)?

Our question has evidently led us far out on a sea of metaphysical speculation, where the shores of practical value and professional preparation have disappeared from view and where we reach toward the limits of what can be intelligibly put into language. Furthermore, even if we wanted to pursue the question for curiosity's sake, it is clear that it is strictly unanswerable. Any possible explanation of how a particular state of affairs causes something, anything, to exist would presuppose the existence of that state of affairs—and so beg the question. The existence of something is a necessary assumption in our talking and thinking about whatever; its ultimate *why*, though, appears to be equally necessarily shrouded in darkness. Surely, therefore, we should guard ourselves from this question that draws us into obscurity, as from a siren's song, and head home to the firm land of our practical pursuits.

But perhaps there is an important lesson to be learned by treading in these waters a moment longer. The question of existence may be unanswerable, but it is also inevitable in our quest to understand our lives. Why are we here? is a hardly unfamiliar cliché that points to something everyone recognizes. It evokes what Heidegger (1953/1996) calls our "thrownness," our condition of being thrown into being, into a strange life we never made (pp. 127–129). We never completely outgrow this condition, however much we try to own our lives, since it is continuous with our sense of mortality that warns we are eventually going to be thrown out. Irrespective of whether the question links easily to our practical cares, or even whether it has an answer, then, it expresses the fact that by virtue of existing at all, we exist, in some essential manner, as ignorant strangers. The land of our practical pursuits can never truly be a home we settle in; we will always be travelers passing through.

Coming back to our Chicago classroom, then, picture a motley crew of would-be specialists thrown together, which provokes them to question why they are there. Now imagine that the teacher manages to get them to wonder about this in existential terms. How he accomplishes this is something we will examine later. The point is that a question, however inchoate and unstated, that initially expressed criticism of our patent, clashing diversity is gradually turned by Jackson, I am suggesting, into one that acknowledges our common condition of being—what I shall call our strangerhood.

How should we respond to this sense that simply to be is to be a stranger? I can think of at least three possible ways. The first would be to flatly deny it. Just as one could suppress doubts about the rationale for this class by noting that it is a requirement and that some more enlightened authority must have a purpose in throwing us into it, so one could insist that there must be some natural or supernatural reason for why we are here. Even if we do not know the reason, and accept the likelihood that we will never know, its postulation permits us to feel at home in being. Now the problem here is not at all that someone may be inclined to trust in some such sense of cosmic meaning. Living by such trust is arguably a kind of wisdom. It comes when one mistakes this faith for knowledge and in the name of a fantasized certainty represses one's own experience of strangerhood. The latter may well not be the last word about one's condition. It is, however, the first rooted in one's actual way of being; it should not be whitewashed in the name of a hypothetical, unexperienced understanding. Faith may encourage the stranger, but dogmatism is for self-deluding occupiers.

A second possible way of responding to our strangerhood amounts to a more partial kind of denial. Rather than completely repressing the experienced fact of our existential condition, it refuses to admit this condition's full implications. We react to the condition as something we can somehow escape; we abandon ourselves to dramatic, stereotypically "existentialist" outbursts of anguish and despair, underscoring our assumption that the condition is a pathology to be suffered until normality returns. Indeed, the more hopeless the abyss of alienation looks, the more furiously we might protest its cosmic injustice. But suppose we took in fully the fact that we are from birth until death strangers to this existing world. Such impulsive gestures, although initially understandable given our familial and historical myths of home, should then give way to a more serious, collected response to our true nature.

What we want, then, is a way of responding to our strangerhood that neither pretends it is not there nor complains about it. This third way would rather strive to live with it, authentically. How is this possible? We would have to discover how to integrate our strangerhood with our other experiences of people, things, and the world. This would constitute an understanding of how various experiences in the world can lead to wonder at existence and how the latter can guide one to better, more satisfying and meaningful experiences in the world. For example, I realize that someone's pronounced shyness reminds me of what it is like to exist, and that this in turn helps me to better savor my experiences of travel. In discerning such connections, I make my strangerhood central to my selfhood and establish that I am most myself when I am in touch with sheer being. This does not mean that I spend the whole day in contemplation, only that I periodically return to the experience of strangerhood because it helps me coherently weave together my past experiences and orients them to a future that better than other alternatives promises to fulfill them.

No one is born knowing how to do this; we all have to learn. I call the work of this self-understanding existential learning. This learning involves coming to understand our experiences in their connection to our strangerhood, deriving from this understanding judgments about how to live, and self-consciously identifying with a community informed by the same interest in this understanding. It may take place haphazardly, or it may also be deliberately cultivated under the guidance of a teacher and nourished by conversation with other students. Naturally, such teachers and students are often found outside of schools. Jackson's teaching, I have come to appreciate, offers us a model of how to cultivate existential learning inside them.

The key to this teaching is recalling the student to the pivotal experience of existential learning: that of strangerhood. Does this mean that the teaching's subject matter is restricted to ontology? Not at all. I explained above that the sense of our strangerhood grows out of facing up to the fact of existence that is absolutely necessary yet unfathomably absurd. Are there not other facts we also more or less necessarily assume that, when we reflect on them, appear more or less essential to our ways of life, to the point where we could hardly think of rejecting them—yet that we also have to acknowledge are at bottom questionable? Consider, for instance, how automatically we take for granted that we are not dreaming, or that we have free will, or that we must be moral. As we know, there is a compelling tradition of philosophical skepticism that contends these are not so much verifiable facts as presuppositions we cannot help but rely on. Now imagine, for a moment, seriously wondering whether the beliefs from which we are bound to proceed are not potentially misleading, whether we are not actually lost. Would not the world formed by doubt of such basic assumptions appear radically strange indeed—and, in this sense, remind us of our existence as strangers? To recall us to our strangerhood, the teacher does not have to focus strictly on the question of existence. He or she need only direct inquiry less toward problems to be solved and more toward questions about our most fundamental assumptions. Although strangerhood is characteristic of our being, we become aware of it whenever we experience, whether in an inquiry into being or into any other seeming first principle, what the Greeks called aporia.

It would seem I am imagining a Socratic teacher who interrogates students about the presuppositions behind some of their elementary beliefs. This is true, but it is not the complete picture. As the fate of Socrates demonstrates, many people are liable to take questions about the beliefs that make them feel at home in the world to be attacks by a subversive enemy. As long as the source of the questions can be perceived to lie outside, one can mistrust the motives of the questioner. But suppose the questions were authored by the students themselves. Let us imagine a teacher who incited students to raise searching questions about certain material and who guided the articulation of these questions such that they came to concern as well fundamental beliefs in the students' own lives. Explicitly, the questions would be directed away from the students, but implicitly, they would boomerang home to roost before any accusations of impiety could even get off the ground.

Certain material: I am plainly thinking of the kinds of texts typical of Jackson's classes. I characterized them initially in negative terms as not contemporary and not taking up education as a central topic. Now we can consider some positive reasons for these features, beginning with the first. The texts come from the past because the teacher can use their historical distance to enhance their provocative power in the present. Earlier, I started to generalize from Jackson's interest in writers like Wittgenstein, Emerson, and Coleridge to virtually the entire range of humanistic and artistic work; we may say that all such work presents us with an understanding of some part of human life. Selecting from this spectrum texts that are rooted in far-off times and places makes it more difficult for us readers to reconstruct what their authors intended to say about human life, particularly if we are not ready to conduct a historical inquiry. The meaning of the text for its author, then, is a question that its historical distance renders more difficult to answer. Yet it does not follow, of course, that the text is unintelligible; it can still have meaning for us. We can find in the work a significant understanding of human life, even if it is not exactly the one the author thought he or she was articulating. This understanding, though, is one that is manifestly a co-product of the given writing and our reading; to arrive at it, we have to involve ourselves in a hermeneutic work of interpretation.[1] The more serious and skilled the effort, the richer the understanding. What the historical distance of the text from us is good for, then, is to concentrate us on—an uncharitable critic would say limit us to—such an effort at exegesis, because it deprives us of easy access to the author's own intentions.

What understanding of human experience do we find in this text? This is the central question that the teacher encourages students to ask. Again, it is a question of interpreting the work, not of evaluating it or situating it in a context. In reply, each one of us will have some initial things to say; all of them will be valid, because they straightforwardly report what we have found. Perhaps one sees nothing interesting. As we share these reactions in conversation, however, differences are apt to emerge that call for resolution. Given that we are together reading the same text, that text should be interpretable as having a coherent meaning and we, as a collective subject, should be of one mind about it.[2] We may not in fact be able to agree on what the text is saying, but it is reasonable to shoot for this in principle. To probe the possibility of consensus in our interpretations, then, we will try to check the meaning of the text's main terms as carefully as possible. We will strive to translate these terms accurately into our own language of human understanding.

At first, we translators will find it easiest to settle for rough equivalents, based on forcing the text's understanding of human experience to resemble our own. We will be predisposed to read the text as either agreeing or disagreeing with us in familiar ways. But, of course, the more scrupulous we are, the less satisfied we will be with such self-serving approximations. Our conscience will direct us back to the spots where the text resists our standard ways of talking about what it is talking about and challenges us to represent sensitively and with nuance its alien understanding. Rising to that challenge will require learning its language, becoming bilingual. To accomplish that, we will need to speculate about how our understanding of a particular part of human life may be significantly altered to accommodate a different one. In the process, we may have to consider how some of our most fundamental assumptions about life as a whole could be otherwise. And this entails questioning them.

The question of what the text is saying, then, may serve as a Trojan horse for this one: Why do you assume that such-and-such is the most suitable way to understand this particular experience? Exegesis need not involve this latter question—but an experienced teacher can lead hermeneutic inquiry in a direction that intercepts such basic beliefs. The express project of the class would be to interpret how a particular text, whose authorial intentions are hidden from us, registers part of human experience. But in the process of pursuing this, students would be drawn to question how their own experience might be understood differently and whether their familiarizing assumptions about life, however essential, are not obscuring the truth. Not some suspicious subversive, but their own inner, readerly conscience would thus bring them before their strangerhood.

Suppose, then, this happens. Where does one go from here? To be a stranger in existence—is that not an utterly paralyzing realization? Not if, as I suggested earlier, it is possible to weave this realization together with one's other experiences and generate new hopes; not if one can turn it into an occasion for existential learning. After all, this realization itself has a history composed of other experiences that preceded it; it is bound to be, in turn, displaced by still other experiences that will capture our attention. The question is whether we can learn how to make these transitions less random and disjointed, and more meaningful and developmental. In here, as in most things, practice makes perfect, and by practicing discerning the links between a text's understanding of a particular human experience, our understanding of that experience, and our experience of strangerhood, we become less prone to denying our existential condition. Conversely, by critically discussing how well texts respond to the particular experience while acknowledging our strangerhood, how well relative to other texts put in conversation with it and to how we would respond, we practice affirming that condition as a path to a coherent life. In many respects, the existential learning I am envisioning resembles the traditional, classic texts seminar of liberal learning, its combination of hermeneutic study, communal conversation, and self-examination. The teacher of such a seminar would keep one eye on the richness of human experience represented in the texts and in the students' memories, and the other on the existential mystery of why we are here, looking for opportunities to explore paths of understanding between them.

Hopefully, I have at least started to explain why existential learning is crucial for staying in touch with a central fact of our condition and why Jackson's teaching provides us with a promising way of cultivating that learning. Even if one is persuaded that his teaching is therefore valuable, however, one might continue to have reservations about its value for educators. After all, I have not yet addressed the other notable, negative feature of this teaching: that it focuses on texts that have next to nothing to do with education.

Suppose it does foster existential learning—what relevance does such learning have to the challenges of educational practice? Will knowing how to live out my strangerhood really make a difference to my work as a principal? Can I truly apply that knowledge, gleaned from pondering a Dickinson poem, to the job of gaining more control over my school's admissions process? Although we may have broached a rationale for Jackson's teaching, it seems to rearouse the suspicion that this teaching is more appropriate for a liberal arts college than a school of education.

As mentioned, the common wisdom is that what we require from the latter is detailed, nuts-and-bolts information about how to be an effective educator. Yet imagine a culture whose members assumed that they needed similarly technical knowledge about how to be a friend. If we visited this culture, would we not be struck by the fact that its members evidently understand friendship to be more like an external feat that one admires and imitates than like an internal feeling that one yields to and communicates? Would we not find it odd that for all the work these people are willing to put into becoming skilled at the reified gestures of friendship, for all the schools that crop up to cater to the market for such skills, few people are interested in understanding, let alone savoring, what those gestures express, what it feels like to be a friend? How strong the impulse would be to urge them to reexamine what friendship really is, to check that they have not mistaken it for— education?

Needless to say, I think education is very much like friendship, much more than it is like brain surgery. This becomes clearer when we appreciate that just as human beings are essentially social beings, so they are essentially learning beings. And they are learning beings because they are *beings*; they exist. Existential learning reminds us, in a most visceral way, that education is how we are ourselves, not an optional practice we take up to achieve some ultimately noneducational end. By stimulating and illuminating the existential learning of educators and would-be educators, regardless of their specialty, we root their professional preparations in our fundamental, common condition as strangers. We encourage them to develop their distinctive craft as an individual way of celebrating that condition. In contrast, when we teach technique without any understanding of its intrinsic motivation—not the same as what extrinsic aims they may serve—we tempt them, and others, to associate teaching and learning with going through the motions, like the smiling face dissociated from the sentiment of friendship.

Education begins in existential learning: If there is any plausibility to this claim, then surely teaching that fosters such learning, and roots educational practice in its primal impulse, should have an important role to play in the preparation of all educators. This is my argument in a nutshell for Jackson's teaching and for an approach to philosophy of education in general modeled on his pedagogy. Philosophy of education, like Hesse's (1969) glass bead game, can be practiced and appreciated as a defining ritual for a culture of strangers, rather than as a trivial pursuit distracting us from the crises of the day.

There remain, however, two doubts about this argument that even I have. First, if it does any justice to his teaching, then why did he not offer us students anything like it when we queried him about that teaching? Why, instead, the cryptic silence? My second doubt is more like a deflating certainty I have been holding at bay, knowing I would have to confront it eventually. Given I am pretty sure that Jackson would have serious qualms—to put it mildly—about my existentialist language, why on earth would I want to champion his teaching in those terms? Am I not afraid of distorting, or even betraying, the genuine spirit of his work?[3]

Afraid is hardly the word. But what I find thankfully bracing is precisely Jackson's silence about his teaching, which over the years I have become convinced was, and is, deliberate. This silence is to his teaching what historical distance is to the texts he taught: Both constitute a veil of ignorance drawn over their authors' intentions. Such a veil, I have suggested, is bound to draw from readers a compensatory effort at, and investment in, interpretation. Accordingly, I have considered what his teaching meant to me, why it got to me so deeply. My explanation links what I experienced in his classes with learning what it is like to exist. Although I characterize the latter experience as one of strangerhood, I have faith that I am not alone in it and that there are better and worse ways of living with this condition. To the extent that others can recognize the truth of our strangerhood, and see how Jackson's teaching can help us acknowledge and respond to it, I am hoping that they will affirm with me the value of this teaching, in general and for educators. Even if they do not share my personal gratitude, they may want to explore how the teaching can be extended in new directions and explicated in different languages.

Whenever one of us asked Jackson what he thought the texts under discussion were saying, he would invariably redirect the question to the class or otherwise refuse to answer, often with a look, I swear, that was da-Vinci-esque. Similarly, when we questioned him about his teaching, he would frequently accompany his evasions with an ambiguous smile. He pushed us to read the books in ever more exacting, concrete ways, yet with respect to his own views about what was going on, ironically he taught us not to press, or rather, not to press *him*. Now I can imagine that some of what I have written here, some of my conjectures about the Jackson pedagogical text, will test this Zen-master-ish good humor. But I have to believe that it will persist unruffled—that it will resolutely reflect the question back to me, asking me to take responsibility for what I find this pedagogy means, and daring me to connect that meaning to the springs of my own life.

A Dewey School Episode

Thomas James

SOMEWHERE IN his writings, Philip W. Jackson walks into a classroom and looks at the children around him. He realizes that the adults are up here and the kids down there, in separate worlds. So he gets down on his haunches, eye to eye with them. From there, he proceeds into the deliberations of his essay.

I never cease to be fascinated by this image. One of the nation's most distinguished scholars in the field of education, author of *Life in Classrooms* (1968) and other seminal works, bends down to join the circle of children. I am inspired by the image because it demonstrates his playful, humane approach to the study of education. I am also drawn to the image, indeed drawn into it, because I was one of those children looking back at him. I was a kid in the elementary school class when Phil Jackson came to the University of Chicago in the 1950s and launched his research into classroom life. I write now in hopes that the excavations of an imperfect memory might add something of more than passing interest to his Festschrift.

My family migrated from Wisconsin to Chicago in the early 1950s when my father entered the doctoral program in the Department of Education, where Professor Jackson held his first academic appointment. Starting his life on the farm where our family homesteaded in the 1850s, my dad had been the first of our family ever to go to college. He met my mother at the University of Wisconsin, and they both became teachers. They lived in a succession of towns—Westby, Barron, Augusta, Whitewater—as my dad went from teacher to principal, interrupted by his call to duty as a ship's captain during World War II, then to local superintendent of schools, and then associate state superintendent of schools in Madison. With all these experiences behind him, he sold his house in Madison, moved to Chicago with his wife and six children, and commenced the lowly existence of a graduate student pursuing a doctorate in educational administration. Asked once, with all those children, if he was Catholic, he responded with the sardonic wit characteristic of a Wisconsin farmer, "No, ignorant Protestant."

We were an outsized crew for our Hyde Park apartment. Small at the front, it was long and narrow, railroad-style. I imagine that our downstairs neighbors tired quickly of so many feet, balls, and toys racing back and forth in the long hallway that extended through the entire apartment. I can still remember walking to school with my father. He was tall and determined, leaning forward as he walked, always ahead of us. We were in awe of him, the four of us who were his school-aged children at the time, following the great administrator-chieftain as we threaded through the streets of Hyde Park, his little covey of kids on the way to the local elementary school, and then in our last 2 years to the school in Judd Hall on campus. In those latter years, which I remember best, he would go in one entrance to the Department of Education, and we would enter next door to the university's Laboratory School.

In our family it was called the Dewey School. I have often heard this usage over the years among my colleagues in the field of education. Before I had set foot in the school but had heard my parents talking after dinner about our going there, I thought we would find a meadow with dew on it. In my mind, it was going to be green and full of flowers, sparkling with dewdrops, like a place I remembered next to the creek on our family farm in Wisconsin. The university's gray Gothic buildings quickly dashed my expectations.

If I am to come anywhere near locating one of those children who might have been looking back at Phil Jackson as he entered the classroom, I will have to acknowledge the many confusions, especially the strange feelings about words, that crisscrossed my own childhood experience. Many years later, I understood why we called it the Dewey School, and I gained a better perspective on why my father went to the University of Chicago for a doctorate. Founded at the turn of the 20th century, the school was one of the most famous experiments in teaching and learning that had ever taken place in modern history. The faculty in the Department of Education, even decades after Dewey had left for Columbia, were influential in generating ideas about teaching and learning. They were also widely respected for developing methods of inquiry needed to refine and sustain those ideas. As a child, I had no way of grasping such adult preoccupations, but my own history as a learner was shaped by them in ways I am still trying to understand.

My excavation of childhood memory hits a rich sediment in the year 1957, when I was 9 years old. It was a year of great importance in my life. I knew for sure I was going to be a baseball star someday. I bought the *Yearbook* for 1957, a publication that came out every year with pictures of major events in the world. It was the only year I acquired that book in my entire childhood. I cannot say for sure, but I believe I asked my mother to buy it because the Russians had launched Sputnik, and that changed everything. You could send things into the sky and keep them there. During air raid drills at school, we were instructed to crouch under our desks. From there, I recall peering up at the little lines and pinpoints of light on the tattered shades our teacher pulled down to make darkness.

That year was one of tremendous human migration, adding to a succession of such years since the end of World War II. The effects were visible in our neighborhood and among my own friends, as African Americans had arrived in large numbers from the South to industrial cities in the North. Since our own move from Madison, my child's-eye view had taken in only scattered glimpses of the wider human change. I had seen a White man belt-whip a Black man surrounded by Whites in a vacant lot near 48th and Dorchester. When we first came to Chicago, one of my friends had been a Black kid just up from Alabama. I had gone to Kenny's apartment two or three times for a pancake breakfast on Saturday morning with his family, which was even bigger than ours. Kenny and I had fought together side by side for our baseball mitts when challenged by other kids, both Black and White, on the dusty lots where we played.

One day coming home, I took a wrong turn and got lost in the late afternoon. I walked for a long time, deep into a Black neighborhood. Finally, seeing that it was getting dark, I had the sense to approach a store. The owner, an old Black man, was out front preparing to close up for the night; he immediately guessed my situation and called my parents. He took me inside, kept the store open, and told me funny stories until my father arrived at dusk. Another day, perhaps a year earlier, I had been chased by half a dozen Black kids, who piled up against the door of our apartment building when I slipped in. I will never forget the ferocious calm with which my mother stepped out and told them to go home, which they did. I came to understand that my parents had moved us from Kenwood Elementary School to the Lab School on campus because the glut of new arrivals to the public school had stopped all forward progress in the curriculum. The most immediate effect from my vantage point was that I lost my Black friends.

Leaving behind the chaos of Kenwood Elementary School, I entered the more peaceful and progressive world of the Dewey School. Yet memory tells me it was not so. On the first day I arrived, I had to fight the class bully. He was bigger than I, but I held him off, even pushed him down hard to the ground—or perhaps not, if I refashioned the incident in memory for later comfort. I suppose the place was like any other school more than it was Dewey's school—and it had not been that in decades. School was an aggressive place, roiling with internal conflicts and fight-or-flight decisions.

To make things worse, I was from Wisconsin, a Milwaukee Braves fan stranded in Cubs and White Sox territory. I played Little League baseball that year. I remember walking tall in my pin-striped uniform on the sidewalk from our apartment to Stag Field. I would never have believed that the field was better known for housing the Manhattan Project in World War II than for the athletic prowess that I and my classmates brought to the plate. I was the A-bomb, we all had plenty of aggression to serve up, and it was a big problem that I worshiped Eddie Matthews, Hank Aaron, and Warren Spahn as the Braves advanced to the World Series. It was not okay that the baseball cards I collected were different from those of my teammates and adversaries. The fight with the bully on my first day had stemmed from immediately perceived differences in baseball interests. Other less dramatic altercations were to follow. But I was able to hold my ground and join the class without giving up my loyalties.

It is a testament to the genius of Phil Jackson that the child's world of fear and hope can be found in his works. The school as a cauldron of raw power and furtive self-recognition was something I richly understood in my own experience and later appreciated when I encountered this scholar's work. The games we played took place in a world delineated by streets and hallways, sometimes on well-worn grass, usually without trees. Our favorite inside game, dodgeball, started with the whole class on one side of the gym, except for one person who stood behind the line on the other side. That one person started with a ball in hand and threw it at the class. When he hit someone, that person joined him and took another ball to throw at the others. The game continued as more people were hit and joined the side with the red rubber balls. Eventually, only one person was left standing on the side where the whole class had been, and everyone was throwing balls at him. I had very quick reactions as a child and often ended up being the last one behind the white line against the wall, dodging all the balls thrown by the rest of the class. It should come as no surprise that a pessimistic attitude toward collective action crept into my thinking over the years.

Although the Dewey School exhibited some of the coarser elements one might find in a conventional school in Chicago or other places, it also had powerful features of the kind celebrated in books on progressive education. I remember these features well. We had a garden nearby on campus. I carried my hoe and worked the soil with my classmates. We cooked and sawed, painted and braided, worked in small groups as well as one on one with our teacher and other adults, then circled all together for recitation. With the help of our German teacher—it seemed hilarious to us that Herr Heine had no hair— we composed letters describing our activities to invisible pals across the ocean. We took field trips to the lumberyard and the Museum of Science and Industry. We congregated on the squared stone blocks along Lake Michigan's shore to ask a fisherman how to catch smelt.

These experiences, I realized much later, had their origin in John Dewey's 1895 essay outlining a plan for a laboratory school at the university. Along with its general argument connecting real-life experiences and genuine bonds of productive community life with the growth of children, that essay included pages listing specific activities, one of which was to boil rice. That a philosopher of Dewey's caliber would include such a concrete suggestion in one of his essays is a sign of how deeply he valued the pedagogy of experience. To a teacher with a knack for creating expeditions, boiling rice takes in everything from world history to the agricultural industry, from basic science to culinary arts, from home economics to the challenges of group decision making. We did not boil rice in my class, at least as far as I can remember, but we did prepare food. I pestered my parents with questions about where the ingredients came from, where the leftovers went when we threw them away, and so forth. The point of the Laboratory School was to engage children in the most productive forms of learning that educators could design and then study the processes of teaching and learning, along with the organization of the school itself, so that new and even better forms of learning could be discovered.

I do have some recollection of observers in our classroom studying us. Not of Phil Jackson specifically, who must have been about 30 years old at the time, but of adults besides our teachers who would talk to us occasionally in small groups or individually. They were busy, serious, frizzy-haired types who would arrive unexpectedly and take notes. I was not yet what university communities affectionately call a faculty brat, since my father was still a graduate student, but I would soon become just that when he went to his first academic job after receiving the doctorate. One of the endearing attributes of faculty brats is their penchant for trying to jimmy the data of researchers conducting experiments on them by giving sly answers. I was not capable of such subterfuge at the time, but it is interesting to think about the presence of Phil Jackson in comparison with that of other researchers. Exquisitely trained in the methods of quantitative social science, he would have escaped any such naughtiness by his subjects under study because he turned toward humanistic and open-ended forms of inquiry that allowed him to join the fun. Anyone's equal in the realm of disciplined inquiry, he grasped the point of W. H. Auden's (1975) lines poking fun at academic seriousness:

Thou shalt not sit
With statisticians nor commit
A social science. (p. 225)

Just so, I hold the image of Phil Jackson in my mind, walking into the schoolyard with a ball in his hand, as he characterized himself recently when reminiscing with a group of educational researchers about those critical moments during his many years of fieldwork when children would turn their attention to him with interest instead of caution.

Many other memories of my Lab School years return to mind. Most are as inconsequential as sour milk along the baseboard under the coat pegs. Others, like the movie we saw at the Quandrangle Club about the boy with green hair, remain indelible while the rest fades. When the boy in the movie washed his hair with something wrong and it turned green, the other kids harassed him. The adults shaved his head to solve the problem, and this made the situation even more embarrassing. Our object lesson was that it is wrong to bully other people. But for me, a confusion about words again entered the picture, no doubt the unavoidable side effect of living in a university community where people routinely deployed multisyllabic Latinate terminology in conversation. After talking with the teacher and then with my parents about the movie, I had some problems with *penalize* and *ostracize*, two words I had heard but could not read. On reflection, it seemed to me that both resulted from doing something bad. The difference was that boys are penalized and girls are ostracized. Along with a short-lived paranoia about shampoo, a certain sqeamishness about these two words formed part of my interior life for several years.

The most consequential memory from my years at the Lab School is the episode for which this essay is named. In all truth, I find it difficult to tell the story because the act of recollection must reach into one of the darkest periods of my life. I press on because I know that the light brought to my situation by the school, particularly by the philosophy of education that gave rise to its methods, makes it well worth the struggle to excavate yet further. I am guided by lines in that same 1895 essay by Dewey. He declared that the school as an institution "must have a *community* of spirit and end realized through *diversity* of powers and acts. Only in this way can it get an organic character, involving reciprocal interdependence" (EW.5.225). I learned firsthand the ways in which a school can become a community that deeply leverages the experiences of childhood for the sake of future growth and happiness.

In the winter of this particular year that I have been calling back from memory, I was invited to go skiing by a friend whose family had a vacation house in Michigan. On my first run down the hill, having never been on skis before, I took a terrible fall. Another person behind me also lost control, and his skis smashed full force into my exposed ankle. Ferried down the slope on a sled litter, I heard someone say that I had broken my leg. Most of the details of what followed are lost to me now, but I recall that the doctors were worried that the break might have been in the place where my bone needed to grow, and it was possible that I would have legs of different lengths. Much more immediately worrisome in the days and weeks that followed was the burden of getting around on crutches with a full leg cast and sore armpits.

Going up and down stairs in the school building was impossible now. Suddenly, I was distant from my classroom and classmates, inhabiting another world known only to the disabled. In more ways than I can possibly describe, things changed in my outlook on life. Darkness in the light shaft behind my bedroom window, pale shadows extending across the streets in those short days, the half-light of corridors inside the university's gray stone buildings—these images remain with me years later, punctuated by bright spots of human affection such as the trip to Marshall Fields with my mother to buy an album for my stamp collection. My grandmother came to visit from Viroqua, outlined my hand in pencil on a piece of paper, and knit me some new mittens. My father let me sit at his rolltop desk, where he studied at the front of the apartment, even if I mixed up his piles of German vocabulary cards. At school, though, the teachers seemed distant and indistinct, the daily schedule all jumbled, friends strangely absent.

There was an old man who worked in the ball room at the Lab School. His place was the best place there was, the logistics center of the school. Chucky Ford was the ball man, and he carried the keys to every room. We called him Chucky, but we knew he was important. He had balls and bats, jump ropes and chalk, all the equipage of recess. He had tools and supplies, the paraphernalia of a progressive school in action. In many ways, he was the glue of the community. Most of the teachers talked with him every day. He was in and out of classrooms, on the playing field, in the gym. He knew every kid in the school. When he found me one morning as I came into the building on my crutches, he asked me to be his assistant in the ball room.

I had my cast on for more than 3 months. For much of that time, I was assigned to Chucky's room. Teachers came and went to bring me things, and I could do my schoolwork there. When I became slightly more mobile, I made some of the rounds with Chucky. Looking back at those months nearly 50 years later, I realize that my experience in the ball room formed a big part of my childhood. Being with Chucky Ford, having the teachers come there, talking about things going on in class and also about things not at all connected with the curriculum, and seeing how the whole school worked from the inside became an incomparable expedition for me.

Something of the community spirit mentioned in the quote from Dewey became apparent to me in learning how Chucky participated in organizing the activities of the school. We talked all the time, and he brought me in as his partner by making it clear to me that he needed my help. We had to get materials out to the playground and into classrooms, and we designed schedules and systems for doing that. Chucky enlisted me in monitoring how things were used and making notes for future occasions, and we would talk about what happened and how the games changed, noting whether there was a need for less rope, more balls, or other equipment.

He knew how to add delight to these tasks. I remember that he would sometimes alter the order of things unpredictably, see what happened with the games kids played, and then discuss it with me. For example, instead of giving the smaller balls to kindergartners, we gave them the biggest ones possible and watched how they used them. More and more, as I learned how the ball room was organized, Chucky asked me to help plan for activities in which the students were engaged. I took some pleasure in this power because whatever the teachers might think, we controlled the equipment. He was funny and cantankerous, faux difficult in the ways that old men can be when they are instinctively kind at the core, a quality also attributed to Phil Jackson by his students.

Organizational acumen learned in the ball room cropped up again in my life when, as a teenager, I planned camping trips in the Sierras after we moved to California. I became logistics-minded as a result of my lucky apprenticeship to the ball man. I learned to plan an extended series of activities, always trying to find the natural order of the expedition, the child's logic of the game, which was the craft wisdom that Chucky carried. I never learned the craft to my full satisfaction, but my experiences gave me a sense of what it meant, as Dewey put it in *Experience and Education* (LW.13), to select experiences that will live fruitfully in future experience.

Many of the topics we discussed in the ball room were drawn from my own life, whether past, present, or future. Chucky discovered in our conversations that both my parents smoked. I cannot recall whether I had formed any judgment of the habit, but I was certainly aware of it in all aspects of my life. Chucky formulated the following problem for me, which I worked hard to solve. If I were to smoke for the rest of my life from age 9 forward, and if I lived to an average age for human beings—a figure he told me I could discover by looking in an almanac—how many cigarettes would I smoke and how much would it cost me over my lifetime? Taking on the problem without complications such as price increases and taxes, I figured it out. At my young age, the number was stupifyingly large. When we looked at it together and checked the math, it was more money than I could imagine ever possessing.

That exercise factored into my own life, I suppose, when I managed never to become a smoker. I was grateful years later when my parents gave up the habit. From a wider perspective, I learned that there is an economy to the things we do—how much we eat, what we decide to spend our money on, the patterns of use for automobiles and all things necessary and unnecessary, even the quality of information we introduce into our lives day by day. Everything carried into our experience forms a lived economy that helps to organize the experiences we are going to have, and the result is our experiential continuum, as Dewey posited the learning process. Chucky Ford taught me that we can illuminate our own experiential continuum through the kind of experiment I conducted with the cost of smoking. We are capable of figuring out how something we do takes shape in our lives. Extrapolating from that lesson in my own life, I came to believe that to the extent we can understand our lives through experience and reflection, we have the power to create worthy experiences, indeed a worthy society if we work together toward that end, and this is education.

I will draw only one more example from my time as apprentice to the ball man. It has to do with the chagrin of being injured as I was. Besides not being able to play baseball in the spring, since my ankle would be too weak even when the cast was removed, a more immediate exile was my inability to participate in snow fights. This was a monumentally serious problem in my midwestern childhood. It was even more serious when one took into account the layout of Hyde Park. Along the southern side of the university, across from our school, lay the midway designed by Frederick Law Olmstead. The midway consisted of entire city blocks left open in grass, including sunken areas flooded in winter for skating. Big snows, frequent in Chicago, meant big snow fights. Teachers would turn their students out for recess, and the fun would begin. Extra minutes, even an hour, might be added after the battle commenced. Teachers joined in, and we had epic snow battles between the grades.

I was in the ball room on a couple of these occasions during that year. When this happened, I felt a sadness more profound than any I had known before. The only respite was conversation. One of the things that Chucky and I often talked about was war. I was keenly interested in the topic, especially my father's war memories from the 1940s and what I had heard about the recently fought Korean War. Chucky and I discussed war strategy, and he mentioned other wars in history. I believe he must have planted the suggestion in my mind that there could be some strategy, even though I was not able to move around much with my cast, by which I could be useful in a snow fight.

Thinking of later developments in my life, I know that this was the first opportunity I had to discover the truth of Kurt Hahn's observation that a disability can become an opportunity (James, 1990). The founder of Outward Bound and other educational organizations meant by this that your limitations can serve as the basis for growth, for going much further than you ever thought you could go as a human being, and the first challenge is to expand your sense of what is possible. Recognizing my immobility, I emerged from my conversations with Chucky Ford with an idea, a strategy. I could become the back of the phalanx, the artillery man in the snow fight. I could be the one who was forming and stacking the snowballs, getting them ready. I would have people working around me in an organized manner, packing and throwing. Following that strategy, the fourth grade could whip the fifth grade.

Out on the midway, I stood at the rear of the column, along with three or four other snowball makers. My cast was flung out to the side as I leaned down, scooped up snow, and formed the balls as fast as I could. Since I couldn't move much, I devoted myself to making as many of them as humanly possible. With efficient reloading from the back and coordinated throwing at the front, we beat the fifth grade that day. In the chaos of battle and the exhilaration of all that released energy in late winter, it is possible that both grades left the field with the impression that they had won, but this was of no consequence. When I arrived home that evening, my cast had gotten so wet that it collapsed as I sat down. I had to go to the hospital to have it replaced. Even that crisis took away none of the taste of victory.

As an educator looking back on my own education, I see that the school was working in subtle ways to live up to Dewey's hope that it embody the spirit of community. If I could go back and investigate the school from an adult perspective, perhaps I might think otherwise. I might come to the conclusion that a progressive school of any authentic kind no longer existed at the Lab School. My own experience, though, especially my conversations with Chucky Ford, demonstrated that it is possible to teach a mode of reflection about the nature of social activity. Ordinary human beings—like an old guy in the ball room—can help adults and children discover how experience can be organized in an enlightened manner as part of schooling.

This one man, taking initiative on my behalf, much as my parents would have wished any school to do, helped me to place myself within that process of experience and reflection in creative ways. But I know his act was not merely individual altruism. It was part of an ethic of caring in the life of the school. That ethic, I am sure, drew others into roles of support when my own needs became apparent. Nor was this caring in an exclusively emotional sense. The invention of a setting tailored to my learning needs represented a whole institution organized to act on behalf of learners with different needs—in my case, an individual who had become disabled, who was cut off from the curriculum, immobilized in a way that kept me out of places where the formal learning was talking place in the school. A convergence of many adults—not just Chucky himself, I suspect—figured out how to form a plan of education around the need my unfortunate situation presented. They gave me opportunities as a learner in a most unexpected way, allowing me to continue my education in the school whose stairs had become impassable to me. Even more than that, I was able to learn in new ways that I had never experienced before, thus reinforcing the excitement of learning itself.

At least in my own personal history, here was a school that discovered the interests of the child, as Dewey had envisioned, and was able to reach those interests through unconventional means if necessary. Phil Jackson came into this world as an observer when he began crouching down and trying to understand these kids and their teachers, both in the Lab School and in other more conventional schools. In the next stage of his career after his research for *Life in Classrooms*, Jackson became principal of the Lab School while also serving as professor and continuing his scholarship and teaching in the Department of Education. I don't know exactly how he conducted his research in schools, but I have read most of his books over the years as my adult life impelled me into the study of education. It was not until his retirement and a conference in his honor that the episode with Chucky Ford fully resurfaced in my mind. I know intuitively that such a history would have been fully recognizable in the young scholar's eyes if at some point I were indeed standing there before him, a child's eyes looking back.

I have used *Life in Classrooms* with my students in more than one university where I have worked as a professor of education over the past two decades. It has always been interesting to watch the reactions. My students, some of whom have gone on to become educational scholars and leaders in their own right, generally could not contain their perplexity on first encounter. They were often taken aback by the book as they saw the unfettered crosscurrents of human nature that the study reveals as it explores classroom life. Yet they were also drawn to some kind of faith it offers about the possibilities for teaching and learning in formal settings we call schools.

To invoke a faith in education does not make it any easier to understand the lifelong work of this scholar. I sometimes would assign my students one of Flannery O'Connor's stories alongside Phil Jackson's writings. For me, the parallels are benighted human experience and a yearning for what should be there. In O'Connor's work the difficulty comes with the gaping absence of any sign of divine grace while knowing that its presence is everywhere and inextinguishable. The world is portrayed as disastrously lacking it, but the stories impel the reader into confronting that presence in its immensity as a response to the illusions and imperfections making up human lives.

It seems to me that Phil Jackson's sense of duty as a scholar is all bound up in struggling against the obstacles blocking the potential for teaching and learning. He knows that learning and human development are precisely what human beings are best designed to accomplish. Yet the world of education he observes is characterized by a woeful lack of clarity and light. He rails against that absence in school and society. Within the academy, he struggles against the methods and disciplinary boundaries that prevent him from formulating the problem in creative ways. Irrepressibly humane, he dares to make his own method, bending social science back toward philosophy, whence it came.

As an educator, Phil Jackson is like Flannery O'Connor in the sense that he is a person with a strong faith in education living in a world with still today so little light to shed on what it means to teach and to learn. I tell my students that *Life in Classrooms* is a classic in the literature on education and that we return to it because the difficulty of understanding schooling processes is where we must begin. Phil Jackson taught us that the desire to illuminate what we do not understand must be stronger than the latest adult logic for explaining away what remains beyond our understanding. This stance pays off handsomely for lifelong students of education, and is the true basis for educational research, when we realize that what we are looking at in schools, classrooms, and children is truly infinite and that no one experiences that infinitude more acutely than the developing child.

When I try to understand my experiences in the ball room in light of my appreciation for what Phil Jackson has contributed to the study of education, another connection comes to mind besides the stories of Flannery O'Connor. This reference, too, is worlds away from the classrooms where the scholar and I might have encountered one another half a century ago. At the end of my college years, I read Igor Stravinsky's (1942/1970) *Poetics of Music in the Form of Six Lessons*. Several parts of that book came to be ever-present in my thinking as I puzzled over the meaning of my own education. Stravinsky talks about a kind of appetite he developed as a composer, an appetite for creation brought on by the foretaste of discovery. Once composers acquire that appetite through creative work, once they learn in their own lives how to seek that foretaste of discovery, then, as Stravinsky suggests, the experience causes them to bring order at the highest level to their efforts. So powerful is the effect of this experience on composers—and, I would argue, on teachers and learners in Phil Jackson's world—that it impels them into continually seeking more discovery and invention throughout their lives.

What Phil Jackson has done for educational research is to initiate a poetics of teaching. His work imparts the foretaste of discovery and leaves that sensation active in the lives of those touched by it. Pleasurable though it may be, no one can rest easily with such an achievement. The appetite for creation is much greater than any knowledge we presently have, or will have. If that appetite is ever lost to certainty, if we conclude that we know what works, the research enterprise will be dead, classrooms deadly, and children even more fugitive than they are now.

CHAPTER 8

The Circus Animals' Desertion: Lessons for Leaders in the Work of Philip W. Jackson

Mary Erina Driscoll

S OME PEOPLE approach a visit to an art museum the same way they would a trip to Europe. See as much as you can, spend a little time in a lot of places, and linger nowhere. They begin a whirlwind journey among the most ancient artifacts and, with or without the headphones and audio guide, progress towards the 21st century at whatever speed their allotted time will permit. Others (and I must confess myself among them) customarily engage in a slightly altered version of artistic tourism: start with some selective list of the museum's "greatest hits," often derived from one's past experiences with favorite exhibits, and make sure that you visit, even briefly, as many of them as you are able every time you come.

But it is a lucky individual indeed who has the opportunity of visiting a museum with Philip Jackson. It's not so much that one does *not* do the kinds of things mentioned above. What is much more interesting is what one *does*. In the case of my most recent visit with Jackson to the Metropolitan Museum of Art, now some years ago, we proceeded immediately through the labyrinth of galleries to a remote installation that he had already seen on many previous outings. We positioned ourselves on a bench in comfortable view of a canvas by Gustav Klimt (an oil painting of a young girl dating from 1912 entitled *Portrait of Mada Primavesi*). We sat for several minutes before the work, each of us studying it intently at first, without comment. Soon, Jackson was asking me questions, some of which seemed spontaneous. Other queries were clearly drawn from his long-standing interest in the work and remained matters of some ambivalence for him despite these earlier experiences. What do you see? What do you think about the objects at her feet? What are we to make of how her arm is positioned? Each question was followed by renewed observation, sometimes discussion. While Jackson's careful and considered reflection had already yielded for him a deep appreciation of this work, it was also apparent that Jackson thought my new eyes might see something that he had overlooked or, perhaps, had long settled in another direction. As we continued to look closely at the painting, we talked at length not only about what we saw but also about what is not there—the perimeter of darkness, to borrow a phrase that is found in Thomas James's essay (Chapter 7, this volume). By the time we left, I had seen far more in this one painting that I had ever found in my previous masterpiece tours.

I have been reminded of this experience in trying to decipher images of educational leadership in Jackson's scholarly work. My task, as I see it, is to probe Jackson's scholarship for insights that are useful to those who study and serve in educational leadership roles. This seems a reasonable project for at least three reasons.

First, I think it is logical to suppose that a theorist who has had such enormous influence on the ways that we understand schools and teaching has something to say of value to the other professionals, among them principals, who work in those settings. Perhaps the task is no more complicated that establishing once again the usefulness of his work for those educators who do not spend their entire professional life in classrooms.

Second, knowing that Jackson himself has been an administrator of a private school serving primary, elementary, and secondary students, as well as a dean of a School of Education, I thought it possible that he might have some useful reflections to share about these experiences. His oeuvre concerning administration directly is slim, numbering roughly one publication, according to my calculations. But could I pass on the opportunity to see how the scholar and the practitioner spoke in this one piece? Finally, there is a third, more personal reason I took on this task. I have been a student of Jackson's and long admirer of his work while a professor and scholar, but, unlike many of the others who cite him, I am grounded in the professional perspective of the field traditionally known as educational administration. To be frank, I welcomed the opportunity to make more explicit for myself and for others the connections between Jackson's work and my field that I believe to be so valuable but that I have never expressed in any systematic fashion.

My experience in the museum came to mind, however, when I began this modest project. What I had perceived to be a straightforward analysis—to focus clearly on what might be an interesting, albeit minor, theme in Jackson's work—became a maddeningly complex task. I had narrowed my scope of vision in the Met to a single painting by Gustav Klimt and found that such singular attention yielded far deeper appreciation than I had thought possible. In this experience, I learned that reading Jackson on this one topic meant I would need to concentrate not only on what he had written but also to make meaning of what was *not* there, for in that, too, significance can be found.

The title of this essay chronicling my efforts is meant to suggest this process, which I found to be alternately frustrating and illuminating. The reference, of course, is to one of the last poems of William Butler Yeats. Throughout his career, Yeats (1956) had embraced many themes and symbols as poetic devices—those "circus animals" he had invented and embellished over time to capture his most essential ideas. But late in life, seeing that "Players and painted stage took all my love / And not those things that they were emblems of" (p. 336), the poet vows to return to the source of his inspiration: "I must lie down where all the ladders start / In the foul rag and bone shop of the heart" (p. 336).

In many ways, Jackson's work is rooted in the rag and bone shop of the classroom, in the most elemental realities that shape schools and children's lives in them. To this he has brought an exquisite Deweyan framework of perception, reflection, and meaning-making, all of which has allowed him to see and to show us what lies beyond our first glimpse of the obvious. To convey the value of this important work for those who try to understand how leadership in schools shapes lives as well, however, required that I dispense with anything that looked like the usual vocabulary of leadership theory. The circus animals that populate our discourse on educational administration and policy—constructs such as instructional leadership, school climate, leadership style, or accountability—were not to be found in any guise. But much was there that offered real wisdom to those who would study and understand leadership in schools. Ironically, I realized that in seeking guidance from his work, I was in some respect looking "outside" my field in order to understand leadership better. In this, of course, my example was none other than Jackson, whose own careful explorations and expositions of work seemingly outside his territory of education have been so invaluable.

This piece is divided, somewhat unequally, into three sections that roughly parallel the process of discovery I experienced on this journey. In the first section I report quite generally about what I saw as Jackson's commentaries on leadership in schools. It should be interpreted as a quick take on what Jackson has to say directly about leadership in the major pieces of school-based research that are so well known. (I do not suggest that my search of his voluminous work has been exhaustive, and offer the caveat that I may have missed some insights.) In the second section, I turn to his autobiographical descriptions of life as an administrator, focusing on a single article. Finally, I take as texts three portraits of schools that were published over 25 years ago in the journal *Daedalus*. It is to these last that I shall devote the most time, as I find in them both embryonic lessons and challenging questions for the field.

JACKSON ON EDUCATIONAL LEADERSHIP: WHAT'S THERE?

My first attempt to address this topic began, as one might expect, with at least a quick review of Jackson's work since *Life in Classrooms* (1968). I focused in particular on his books and on a selection of articles that have been published only in journal form. It was by no means a comprehensive cataloguing of all that he has written (and such was not my intention). I wanted, rather, to take a sounding, to establish how deep were his observations about school leaders, to see what he thought about their importance—indeed, to figure out if, in his view, they matter at all.

Having dropped my lead, what I found did not surprise me: Most, if not all, of Jackson's work does not focus directly on school administrators. And as his work has developed, his lessons are ever tied less and less to those working in schools and more to the project of education in general. Despite these constraints, however, there was still some justification for further pursuit. Jackson's work includes two major books based on classroom and teacher observations and interviews—*Life in Classrooms* (Jackson, 1968) and *The Moral Life of Schools* (Jackson, Boostrom, & Hansen, 1993). With so much time spent in schools, I reasoned, even a perspective focused on the classroom would surely include some observations about the leaders who appear, if only in supporting roles. If Jackson's sights were fixed on teachers and classrooms, I suspected, then the people who helped to run the schools that housed those classrooms must be found in the latitudes not too far removed from this center.

Upon rereading, I found (to no great surprise) that *Life in Classrooms* is just that: a book focused almost entirely on classroom life, with little to no interruption from principals, assistant principals, or anyone of that ilk. Principals do not figure in the main data, nor do they even merit an entry in the index. Administrators do eventually emerge in the interviews Jackson does with teachers, but they are barely named as such, presented as an amorphous "they" in some teacher accounts. Indeed, most of these references focus on teachers' desires to keep "them" out of their classrooms, especially if "they" are taking notes. There are some observations about the degree to which teachers perceive intrusions on their curricular freedom (again by unnamed administrative types) as formidable threats. But the designated school leaders remain very much in the background, if not the shadows, of the book.

Fair enough, I thought; when this was written, Jackson was making the transition from "pure" psychology to the Jackson he would become (as Lee Shulman so elegantly puts it in Chapter 1 of this volume). I turned again to *The Moral Life of Schools*, with modestly increased expectations of seeing a view broader than just the classroom. By the time this project was undertaken, Jackson had completed his own administrative career, and the notion that ideas of moral schools as well as classrooms would be portrayed seemed reasonable. Surely, I would find a principal or two here.

Indeed, in the first sentence of the preface, Jackson and colleagues name administrators (among several other groups) as an intended audience for their book. But the authors quickly go on to explain that despite the title, the focus of the piece will remain classrooms, for they "form the heart of the school" and must be the starting place for understanding its moral life. Whether or not administrators study the moral implications of their own actions, we learn, it is vital that they reflect on what happens in classrooms, for life in classrooms remains the true center of the enterprise.

This perspective is confirmed when one searches the book's descriptions of classroom activity and teacher interviews, not to mention its index, for the presence of the positional leader in these schools. It would be hard to sketch them even as minor characters; not once by my count, for example, does a principal visit a room described, nor does the intercom interrupt with exhortations or instructions, moral or otherwise. No child is sent to the principal; no teacher complains in this text about intrusive administration. The message is clear: It is not through administrators that we understand the moral life of schools. Moreover, it is possible to learn a great deal about that life without even bringing them into the picture.

What I suspected to be true, at least with respect to these two pieces, seemed now to be firmly established. A significant researcher and theorist, one known for capturing in fine grain the life of classrooms and schools, whose work drew from the lived experience of those places, simply was not noticing administrators. Of course, what we read in these texts is the equivalent of the director's cut: It may be that research notes, interviews, observations, and logs contain more information than we are shown in this version. But that too is telling, for if true, it would imply that the administrator's presence in these classrooms that are so carefully watched is so minor it does not merit mention.

Seeing what is *not* there in these texts, in other words, tells us a story. And I think the story being told is simply that what *is* there—that is, rich descriptions of, and reflections on, children's experiences and the work of those who teach them—is by far the most important thing going on in any school. The search for factors affecting those experiences is all centered on the smallest units—on the classroom, on the children themselves, and on the experiences and insights of the teachers whose own lived reality bears understanding and reflection as well.

I do not wish to belabor this point, but I think it is an important one. At the present time, educational policy seems dominated by the belief that leadership is the central engine of the school and the best and surest key to school improvement. Toward that end, major philanthropic efforts have been developed to educate (and reeducate) this generation of school principals. Costly policy battles have been waged to make it easier to remove substandard leaders and to increase the autonomy of good ones (provided, of course, there is appropriate accountability). Principals are exhorted to become instructional leaders, driving important decisions with their assessment data. In the current administrative canon (not to mention the conventions that now dominate principal selection) it would be unthinkable to imagine a school leader who did not have a "vision" and unbelievable to assert that that vision should not pervade every classroom in the school to its very floorboards. In short, my exercise thus far suggests that by focusing too much on the titular head of schools, current policy has succeeded in yet another failed version of the "engineering" of schools of which Jackson was so suspicious in *Life in Classrooms*.

I have deliberately painted the field with a broad brush, and certainly there are many in the field of educational leadership who are in sympathy with the idea that teachers, children, and classrooms should remain the focus of our attention. But it is still humbling and daunting to realize Jackson's lesson. The single most important thing happening in schools is still what occurs on a day-to-day basis between individuals in classrooms, and all educators, be they administrators or not, are wise to remember this fact.

JACKSON AS EDUCATIONAL LEADER

Jackson served as an educational administrator at the University of Chicago Laboratory schools for over 8 years, first as principal of the nursery/lower schools and later as the director of the Laboratory Schools. (His administrative career also included a term as dean when Chicago had a School as well as a Department of Education.) This autobiographical experience forms the basis of a short piece written by Jackson, published in 1977 in the *School*

Review (later called the *American Journal of Education*), entitled "Lonely at the Top."

It is intended to be a slight piece, a first-hand account, and hardly a sweeping statement about the profession itself. But the themes he sounds ring true to today.

The title is drawn from the caption of a Whitney Darrow cartoon in *The New Yorker* that portrays "in comic relief the stereotype of the top administrator—an overweight and balding man in posh surroundings who speaks in clichés about human feelings while clutching the symbols of contrived bonhomie, cards in one hand, booze in the other" (Jackson, 1977, p. 425). How silly, he seems to say as he begins, to imagine loneliness in the midst of such privileged trappings.

But it is to loneliness that he returns more than once in this piece, and to the isolation that school leaders feel on a day-to-day basis, feelings that originate in part from the deep and surprisingly intimate knowledge of the faculty and the school community that comes, often unbidden, to those in leadership positions. (Indeed, the subtitle of the piece is "Observations on the Genesis of Administrative Isolation.") To know and yet not to be able to share such confidence—this, he found, was an abiding reality in his day-to-day life as an administrator.

Interesting, I thought, to focus on this aspect of the job. On reflection, it is more than interesting; it is, rather, an intuitive leap toward what turns out to be an enduring dilemma in the profession. It's worth noting that when this was written, contemporaneous scholars in the field—indeed, at the very institution at which Jackson was employed—were much enamored with the complexities of administration produced by structural imperatives, many of which were vestigial remnants of organizations and purposes no longer current. Similarly, researchers also focused on the "role sets" and structures that constrained and shaped opportunities for interaction and knowledge within an institution. Experience as the director of the University of Chicago Laboratory School, embedded as it was then in the overlapping (and often contradictory) communities of university, research department, and local community, might well have provided an apt opportunity to reflect on such topics. The vocabulary of administrative theory at the time would have pointed some scholars, in other words, in a very different direction.

But Jackson's reflection on Dewey's school made no such claims and needed so such circus animals. Rather than think about the structure and functions of administration in that setting, he hones in on an important and still understudied affective dimension of administrative life. The constant truth of administrative loneliness—produced not only by positional isolation but also by the sense that one is under constant surveillance—is the theme he takes as his starting point, and his brief account can still startle us with its poignancy.

There is another, more muted theme in this piece, one that betrays a certain restiveness with the task Jackson set for himself. Jackson is properly cautious about the first-person nature of his data collection, inserting the appropriate caveats about the degree to which such autobiographical data may generalize to a wider setting. But I think these concerns are less about the empirical half-life of his reflections and more indicative of his consciousness that what he had produced did not look like "traditional" scholarship at the time. In light of Jackson's gradual embrace of the arts in his scholarly writing in the years to follow, this point may be worth some consideration.

Robert Frost's insight about the differences between scholars and artists may be helpful here. "Both work from knowledge," he tells us, "but I suspect they differ most importantly in the way their knowledge is come by." For scholars, Frost continues, knowledge is gained by "conscientious thoroughness along projected lines of logic." But poets get their knowledge "cavalierly and as it happens in and out of books. They stick to nothing deliberately, but let what will stick to them, like burrs as they walk the field. No acquirement is on assignment, or even self-assignment" (1939/1972, pp. 394–395).

The artist learns by "snatching" what he knows from some "previous order in time and space"; not so the school boy, who "may be defined as one who can tell you what he knows in the order in which he learned it" (Frost, 1939/1972, p. 395).

This artistic knowledge-getting that Frost speaks of is at the heart of "Lonely at the Top," I think. Jackson's knowledge, like that of any true scholar-practitioner, is less the product of thoroughness along lines of logic than it is the work of the ever-attentive artist that Frost describes. The burrs of administrative life that stick to Jackson do not remain unexamined, and "Lonely at the Top" provides him with the opportunity to make sense of them. Despite (or perhaps because of) their intuitive nature and affective pull, these "burrs" are transformed into glimmerings of truth that two decades later still seem fresh and wise.

JACKSON ON SITE: LEARNING FROM LEADERS

In the late 1970s, Jackson was part of a project in which three scholars (Jackson, Sara Lawrence Lightfoot, and Theodore Sizer) visited the same three schools. All schools were considered at some level to be "good," although the reader will find in their reports much more of a meditation on what constitutes goodness in schools than a roadmap to educational virtue. The three reports by each scholar were published together in the fall 1981 volume of *Daedalus*. The authors' collective and often contrasting visions of these institutions and what we can learn from them makes for fascinating reading.

They also serve to remind us that well before the shot heard round the world of educational reform known as *A Nation at Risk* (National Commission on Excellence in Education, 1983), serious scholars were engaged in thoughtful assessment of what was occurring in our schools and wondering if "good" was enough.

It's also fun to read the pieces when one knows where these scholars progressed in their thinking during the decade following this project. In Lightfoot's pieces, we see an early version of what would become her signature method, portraiture (e.g., Lightfoot, 1983). In Sizer's work, we see the seeds of the project that began with *Horace's Compromise* (1984) and begat the Coalition for Essential Schools. And in Jackson's essays, we see his thinking when his projects *The Practice of Teaching* (1986) and *The Moral Life of Schools* (Jackson et al., 1993) were still in utero. Still, when reading them we can begin to map the route that will lead in the next two decades not only to these destinations but also from those vantage points to Dewey, Heidegger, and beyond.

I reread these pieces in search of what I had not been able to see in other work: Jackson and living, breathing administrators. No more could they elude him, I hoped, and vice versa. And to varying degrees, each of the school portraits does include some encounter with a school administrator who both becomes part of the portrait and helps Jackson to decipher its lines. Perhaps here, I speculated, Jackson would make even some small comment on how the school leaders he met fit into these ruminations about good schools and how they got there.

What I found in my rereading did not disappoint. As I had come to expect, however, what was there was hardly as obvious as I had hoped. Although some mention of administration appears in each of the three essays, there is only one extended treatment of the role of the principal; taken together, however, they provide varying images of the ways in which administrators shape and give expression to their school's ethos. A final caution: Each of these pieces is a detailed and rich description of the three schools, from which Jackson draws major reflections on the promise of education, the importance of curriculum, and other critical matters. (To find another exposition of these texts, one need look no further than Lauren Sosniak's essay in Chapter 9 of this volume.) What follows, then, is by no means a full reading of these pieces but, rather, some brief impressions of what he tells us about the administrative role in these schools.

In the essay on St Paul's called "Secondary Schooling for the Privileged Few," Jackson (1981c) presents a detailed portrait of one of the most elite New England prep schools, circa 1978. It is a place of great abundance, and from the outset, Jackson chronicles the "surfeit" of resources he encounters, a true embarrassment of educational riches. Among these are the impressive

New England prep school campus, a large staff (both visible and invisible), and the many resources and opportunities available for both athletic and nonathletic co-curricular activities. As a result, St. Paul's is able to attract top students and to offer classes in ways that challenge students with demanding materials. Trying to estimate how the resources he sees stack up to those available to public schools of the time, Jackson calculates that St. Paul's spends roughly four times what the average public school of the day does per pupil. Such wealth makes it clear that although lessons for all schools may be taken from the St. Paul's example, the disparities between this and any other school remain great.

Jackson conveys to us the ability of the school to create the kind of total environment in which the entire institution seems focused on the avowed purposes of the school. The aim of administrators, faculty, and staff is to fuse the ideals of St. Paul's with the very identity of its students. Perhaps because of the magnitude of the resources at their disposal, what emerges (among other things) is an organic image of a school community focused on the growth and development of young people, whose education has been the mission of St. Paul's for over a century. It is in describing this unity of purpose that Jackson's sole reference to the school's administrator (called the rector) emerges. Here, he quotes directly from the rector's address to faculty:

> My first observation is that we are first and foremost an educational institution, organized and supported for the purpose of helping young students grow and develop and mature into strong young adults. Our principal activities are controlled by that primary responsibility. Everything we do—our actions and efforts in class, on the athletic fields, in dormitories, in the dining rooms, in activities—every action everywhere is rooted in this primary responsibility. (quoted in Jackson, 1981c, p. 123)

Although the rector never appears in the essay in any more personal guise, it is his words that punctuate the story Jackson is telling. But it is just that: punctuation. The story is told by the entirety of the place, and the school as Jackson encounters it is suffused with the ideals to which the rector gives voice. "Though the rector states quite explicitly the school's concern for the total development of its students," Jackson comments, "his words do not begin to reveal the mechanisms in which the lives of the students and the life of the school become intertwined" (p. 123). Thus the rector's exhortation to remember the noble aims of St. Paul's in all things is less a clarion call to action than an echo of a theme already well sounded throughout the institution.

It is clear that leadership as such is not a major theme in this essay, but what we do see nicely maps onto the now familiar images of leadership as stewardship (see, e.g., Sergiovanni, 1992). The steward does not own that which is valued—in this case, the idea of what St. Paul's aspires to be in the life of each student. Rather, he is charged on behalf of all concerned to nourish and sustain that vision. It is an organic image of leadership in that leader and school community share such commonalities of beliefs and values that one cannot say with any authority which affect the other more. Indeed, the very notion of organic implies that one has hardly caused the other and that they have grown together in a complex web of relations over time.

Learning from an institution such as St. Paul's is difficult, in part because it presents itself as such a complete entity that it is almost impossible to know its origins. How could a community with similar aspirations achieve like purposes? Do leaders bring such places into being, or are they born from them? To what extent does the traditional authority of a rector lend itself to this type of symbolic leadership, and without the trappings of religion and history, is it possible to imagine a civil servant leader as a steward? Although few if any of these questions may be found directly in the essay, Jackson's analysis of this unique institution prompts their consideration.

If Jackson's story of St. Paul's could be told without making reference to the school's Head, his essay on Carver High School in Atlanta cannot. Norris Hogans is the forceful leader of this troubled high school portrayed in "Secondary Schooling for Children of the Poor" (1981a), and Jackson's accounts of his words and actions dominate the first half of this essay. Hogans and his superintendent, Alonzo Crim, appear early in this piece, and Jackson is careful to announce that in retelling the stories of the school's success that "my own knowledge of that history comes exclusively from informants with a vested interest in the school as it is today—the superintendent of schools, the school's principal, and its current staff—and who therefore might unconsciously paint the present in rosier tones than the past" (1981a, pp. 42-43).

The story he is told (certainly believable "in broad outline," he acknowledges) is one of redemption: Carver has turned in a few short years from a violent and dysfunctional student warehouse into a safe, orderly school. Now Carver enjoys high staff morale and has shown documented progress in student attendance. The administration at Carver has reduced suspensions and the dropout rate, has increased overall enrollment, has improved job and college placement, and has worked to ensure better support from and involvement with the community. Such is their success that prior to Jackson's visit, Crim and Hogans have promoted the "Carver Model" in congressional testimony as a "workable solution" to the endemic problems of large, poor, inner-city schools. The model rests on strategies that take action to restore order, instill pride in students, make community leaders responsible for and to the school, and address curricular deficiencies that disengage students and limit their life chances. Jackson is impressed (if not uniformly charmed) by the forcefulness with which Hogans attacks his mission, so much so that he begins to see that the exportable "strategies" of the Carver model and the man himself are inextricably interwoven:

> The Carver Model, as Hogans likes to call it, is a set of strategies—epitomized maxims such as Involve Parents in the School's Operations, See External Funding, Build a Base of Community Support, and so forth—so simple and straightforward that any sensible administrator faced with similar circumstances might have come up with it. Hogans' accomplishments reflect no blinding insight into the educative process. But the common-sense quality of the notions undergirding his efforts to improve Carver adds to his achievement. For it reminds us that what makes the difference is the ability to make the ideas a reality. And it is this quality in Hogans that elicits our admiration and applause. The Carver Model is none other than Hogans himself. (Jackson, 1981a, p. 48).

Perhaps, Jackson suggests, all one needs to improve a school is such an administrator: "plenty of drive and commitment; the capacity to be warm and friendly, but also the courage to bang a few heads together from time to time and to snarl once in while to get things done; some good ideas but not necessarily new ones; enough *chutspah* to toot his own horn when given a chance; and to top it all, a knack for working The System" (p. 49). Indeed, he continues, "The ultimate Workable Solution to the Problems of Urban Education is to place one such person in the front office of every vocational high school in the land. On that happy day educators and concerned citizens could finally sit back and relax" (1981a, p. 49).

Even a reader unaware of Jackson's earlier work could recognize the irony in this last statement, given the hints he has given us in the essay's opening pages. There Jackson compares his first impression of Carver, a turreted former college building set on a campus that holds an impressive view of Atlanta, to his first impression of Disneyland some years before. "In retrospect," he tells us, "my initial reaction was a harbinger of things to come, and that same feeling of not quite trusting the brightness and the cheerful look of things recurred often enough to be troublesome" (1981a, p. 40).

What Jackson has so quickly recognized at Carver is that he has been presented with a hero's tale of success. The story comes complete with a conquering principal who has vanquished the villains of educational poverty and violence, rescuing Carver in the nick of time. It is an appealing saga and one that has clearly impelled the school community to build this legend.

Hardly a complete fiction, the hero's tale of salvation becomes a story whose sole purpose is to inspire others. As such, it has taken on for those who hear it some of the characteristics that the critic Denis Donoghue attributes to myth. Myths are different from fiction because "we have not invented it; [and] we have received it for its use by other people: in many cases it may already be a force in the world at large" (Donoghue, 1986, p. 22). The power of myths to organize action in others is real. We know this to be true whether we are speaking of the chieftain's sagas that inspired Romantic Ireland (as is Donoghue), or recounting the myriad tales of hero principals turning around schools that have taken on life in the educational policy rhetoric during the three decades since Jackson relayed Hogans's compelling story.

But it is precisely because myths are powerful that they are also dangerous. Myths organize action, but usually in only one intended direction, smoothing over the rough edges that do not enhance the story and consciously excising the uncomfortable realities that trouble their logic and sway. To rely on myth alone is to ignore those things they do not choose to include. Jackson's tantalizing reference to Disneyland early on belies his acknowledgment that the hero's tale, compelling as it may be, can be at best only a part of the solution. It is not so much that Jackson challenges or deconstructs Hogans's story in the second part of this essay. It is more that he returns again to the questioning skepticism that leads directly to the harsh and endemic realities of urban poverty and the paucity of vision in the vocational training promoted as an answer to these problems. The essay includes a tough-minded assessment of the enormity of the issues at hand. This analysis exists side by side with an appealing hero's tale, and it is these probing questions that ultimately outweigh the "solution" offered. I suspect this is why the essay finally takes the form of an examination of some enduring problems in education rather than just the report of a visit to one emblematic case.

Anyone seriously interested in school improvement is wise to both respect and beware the myths of hero principals. To deny their power is unrealistic. The alchemy of their inspirational pull may help to sustain the optimism, commitment, and hard work it takes to meet the daunting challenges of urban schooling. But we must always be aware of the tendency in these stories to simplify, to filter, and to sanitize the very realities they seek to illuminate. To encounter these hard truths requires more than myth: it requires the kind of careful and skeptical analysis that imbues the latter part of this essay.

Finally, what are we to make of the brief appearance of the principal in the third essay in this set, Jackson's analysis of the large suburban school known as Highland Park High School? In "Comprehending a Well-Run Comprehensive: A Report on a Visit to a Large Suburban High School," Jackson (1981b) describes his brief visit to a large institution with an array of curricular offerings so diverse as to be bewildering. Students come from relatively affluent homes, and the school enjoys strong support from the community. Teachers seem satisfied. Resources are plentiful. Jackson finds the staff to be remarkably uniform in their enthusiasm. "When asked about the current state of the school, the answer was always the same," he recounts. "Little problems? Yes. Big problems? No. Compared to other schools in which they had worked or had heard about? No problems at all" (1981b, p. 85).

The general state of satisfaction with the school—what Jackson calls "a recognition of continuing problems combined with a general spirit of contentment"—is very much evident in the conversations with administrators reported by Jackson:

> The school is a smoothly running institution, led by a competent team of administrators and staffed by a conscientious and professional cadre of teachers and counselors. . . . The principal acknowledges that there are some students who "get lost" and "fall through the cracks" of the various programs. He worries about such students, many of whom seem to be transferees from other high schools. He also complains that there are a few weak teachers who are "almost impossible to get rid of," and feels uneasy over the school being "more impersonal and more of an institution" than it once was. . . . At the same time he has high praise for the school as it operates today, claiming that it is "better for kids" than it had been in the past. "It's a better educational program. More is offered by better teachers," he explained. (1981b, p. 85)

From this point on, the essay morphs into an extended reflection on the questionable benefits of the comprehensive curricular structure of the school. Curricular choice is both permitted and constrained by the policies affecting distribution requirements for graduation, and Jackson wonders aloud about the relationship of these particular progressive notions with other ideas about what constitutes a "good" education. Although the construction of such policies is clearly an administrative function, Jackson says little more about the administrators themselves. The genial, slightly worried, but genuinely contented individual cited above remains our chief picture of the "strong leadership" cited by several similarly contented teachers in the school.

I must confess that at this point in my journey—near the end, perhaps, but by now attendant to the slightest nuance in his carefully chosen language—I found myself hearing a note intended but struck every so softly in his account. Terms such as *well-run*, *smoothly*, and *contented* all began to carry a negative connotation, a vague charge of mindless efficiency as one's chief accomplishment. The faint praise runs throughout the description above: administrators are "competent," leading a "conscientious" staff. The image of unthinking, well-organized professionals, diligently ensuring that the educational trains ran on time without ever asking where they were going, was unmistakable. What to make of this?

Still troubled by that image—what are administrators to do, after all, if they are at the helm of a relatively trouble-free school, I wondered—I found myself caught by the following sentences. Jackson confesses that at the end of the first day "the level of my curiosity about the school had sunk to near zero. There was so little that was problematic about its overall workings . . .

everything was so predictable, so understandable, so sensible—and conse-quently, so dull" (1981b, p. 86).

And then it hit me: No one to whom Jackson spoke, most certainly not the principal and, for the most part, not the teachers, appears to be even re-motely curious in this piece. Although the principal worries about the kids who fall between the cracks, he is confident that those who fall within the lines will be all right. The concerns he expresses are all about the exceptions to the norm, and there is little to suggest that the norm itself is ever under scrutiny.

We might expect curiosity as routine behavior from university profes-sors, especially those who have been engaged to visit and write about a school. On final consideration, however, I think it is this last "lesson for leadership" that is the most valuable insight I gleaned. School leaders, whoever they are, should also be curious. Curiosity is simply that: not a code for evaluative scru-tiny, but, rather, a desire to question and to figure out, perhaps initially with-out any notion of where the inquiry may lead. It means asking questions that they don't know the answer to and paying attention in ways that make them notice the things they end up questioning, those burrs of school life that must be picked apart if we are to understand their import. Such activity is not only the way we progress intellectually—recall my earlier story of the museum visit—but it is the only real way, perhaps, to engage a community in dialogue about things that matter.

Curiosity may be unusual, even discouraged, in school leaders, but it is entirely within the realm of possibility. Witness this account of a young ad-ministrator, unfamiliar with the norms of the primary school he found him-self directing, as he tries to make sense of this new world:

> I was a newcomer to both school administration and nursery schools at the time. Consequently, in order to familiarize myself with the institution and how its teachers behaved I spent as much time as I could during my first few weeks on the job poking about the school as a complete stranger might, watching what was going on and trying to get a feel for the place. . . . As the days wore on I slowly became aware of certain things the teachers did that distinguished them from the kinds of teachers I had spent most time with in the past—those with much older pupils. . . . These . . . examples of what seemed to me to be charac-teristic behavior of nursery school teachers so intrigued me that I decided to share my discoveries with the teachers themselves. . . . Broaching the topic over lunch one day, I rather casually announced as though it seemed my observa-tions around school were beginning to pay off.

The novice administrator, of course, is Jackson himself, and this passage from *The Practice of Teaching* (1986, pp. 75–76) continues by describing how a deceptively simple lunchtime conversation between principal and teachers led to far more serious discussion of the how teachers think and what we must learn to become a teacher. "As could be guessed, the teachers and I never did succeed in answering most of the question we so enthusiastically and, I fear, naively wrestled with back then. Nor have I yet done so. But both individually and collectively we did develop some tentative notions about the directions in which a few of the answers might lie" (Jackson, 1986, p. 77).

UNTAUGHT LESSONS

Some lessons, Jackson (1992) tells us, are "untaught" in the sense that they are not "part of the teacher's explicit agenda or lesson plan" (p. xi). I have taken as my topic those untaught lessons on leadership found in a lifetime's work by my teacher Philip W. Jackson. In brief, albeit in most un-Jacksonian form, I would suggest they might read as follows:

Pay attention to the heart of the school, the classroom, and never let other notions of what matters in education overshadow it.

Remember that leaders are shaped by the realities that surround them, and among these one may find both loneliness and a forced isolation from that classroom.

Understand that although a leader may embody a school's dreams for its students, he or she probably shepherds, rather than creates, that vision.

Beware the hero's tale, especially when its allure distracts one from more uncomfortable educational truths.

Above all, be curious, seeking not to name what one knows in the order one learned it, but rather to know and name what one lives in schools. This will require paying attention and will demand participation in an ongoing cycle of questioning and reflection in order to arrive at the next end-in-sight. (This behavior may be practiced, it turns out, when visiting an art museum.)

Individually, each of these lessons is a provocative and intriguing maxim. Collectively, these insights are a powerful warning to the field to keep in sight those things that matter most and, as one struggles with the difficult questions, to remain committed to develop—at the very least—some "tentative notions" about the directions in which a few of the answers might lie.

The Generalist Educator: Making a Mark on Curriculum Studies

Lauren A. Sosniak

OR MANY scholars, education is a rich venue for psychological investigation. So it was for Philip Jackson at the start of his academic career. His strengths and success as an educational psychologist were apparent quickly. His early publications included, for example, *Creativity and Intelligence* (Getzels & Jackson, 1962) and the chapter on "The Teacher's Personality and Characteristics" in the first *Handbook of Research on Teaching* (Getzels & Jackson, 1963). Still, before too long, both the content and the method of psychology apparently lost its allure. Jackson began to transform himself into a more wide-ranging educator: a scholar of teaching, learning, and schooling; a generalist crossing boundaries of psychology, history, sociology, literature, and, especially, philosophy.

Life in Classrooms (1968) is compelling evidence of the early years in this transition. Many people know this book as a groundbreaking moment in methods of educational research, leading a movement that would allow the power and value of qualitative research to stand side by side with that of quantitative work. But Jackson's methodological shift was the least of his contributions to education. Both the substance of the book and its style were groundbreaking.

Anyone who has read the book surely remembers Jackson calling on us to think about "the elements of repetition, redundancy, and ritualistic action" (p. 6) that students experience in classroom. In the same first chapter Jackson reminded us of the "three facts of life with which even the youngest student must learn to deal . . . : crowds, praise, and power" (p. 10). His discussion of the institutional aspects of schooling, so finely and elegantly developed, helped us see classrooms as we knew them but had never quite thought about them before. Never had we attended as deeply, as richly, with all the links and the consequences, to the transitory events that so add up as they are "experienced by millions of persons and by each person millions of times" (p. 177).

Life in Classrooms is not only nor even principally concerned with students' experiences. Jackson broke much ground in research on teaching with his report of interviews with a group of masters of the craft. Jackson helped us think about the lenses through which a group of good teachers viewed their life in the classroom: immediacy, informality, autonomy, and individuality. He called attention to features of the teachers' talk: absence of a technical vocabulary, conceptual simplicity, sharp existential boundaries. Jackson set teacher talk in the context of the extraordinarily active and socially interactive work: "as many as 1000 interpersonal interchanges each day" (p. 11). And Jackson coined the language of "interactive" and "preactive" teaching processes that have helped us think about both the immediate and the planful aspects of teacher responsibilities.

In other words, as far back as 1968, in a small number of pages Jackson offered researchers a large number of conceptual inventions that have reverberated through so many different lines of educational research ever since. And *Life in Classrooms* was just the start of Jackson's contributions to new ways of thinking about teaching, learning, and schooling. Jackson's work for the next many years would sometimes highlight what had always been before us and yet had gone unnoticed, sometimes challenge existing ways of thinking, and sometimes help us deal with long-standing unresolved debates. Typically Jackson has led the way as the world of research on teaching and life in classrooms has expanded substantively and methodologically.

Among the highlights of Jackson's continuing work on teaching, surely we would have to include *The Practice of Teaching* (1986), especially the chapter on "The Mimetic and the Transformative: Alternative Outlooks on Teaching." Here Jackson speaks about competing traditions in teaching with long histories and with distinct meanings for students and teachers. These traditions frequently have been labeled with what have become psychologically loaded names: traditional versus progressive education, subject-centered versus child-centered teaching, or direct instruction versus constructivist teaching. Jackson clearly lays out the essential differences between the two points of view and goes on to examine how, "in the real world," these alternative ways of working tend to be complementary rather than mutually exclusive. Then, for the better or the worse for those of us who hold strong positions, Jackson makes clear that the public debate undoubtedly is much more divisive than students' and teachers' experiences in the classroom; it would be nearly impossible to work entirely one way or the other. There are consequences, however, in emphasizing either the mimetic or the transformative, and Jackson walks us through some of the more serious implications for educational practice and research.

Jackson's work on teaching and schooling has touched so many different communities of educational researchers and is so well known that mere reminders should call to mind for most readers of this volume the richness of his publications and their trajectory. What might be less well known, though, is Jackson's work in the field of curriculum studies. The remainder of this essay is devoted to Jackson's work as a "curricularist," as he has sometimes called it, or, more fundamentally, as a generalist educator.

TEACHING SOMETHING, TO SOMEONE, IN SOME CONTEXT

By the time I was a student at the University of Chicago, in the 1970s and 1980s, Mr. Jackson (as my classmates and I called him in those days) was reading, writing, and teaching literature that went well beyond educational psychology and also well beyond work being done then in the area of research on teaching. All the courses I took with Jackson, which I believe would be all of the courses he taught at that time, included considerable attention to matters of curriculum. Jackson was interested in both curriculum history and its contemporary manifestations. Curriculum studies became my passion because I was introduced to the field by Phil Jackson.

Perhaps Jackson gravitated to curriculum studies because of the historical power of his university in this field of study and the Chicago influence on Jackson as well. After all, Chicago was home to Dewey, Bobbitt, Tyler, Schwab, and so many others who have left their mark on the field. But maybe it was something different.

In 2003, at an American Educational Research Association (AERA) symposium titled "Becoming a Scholar of Curriculum," Jackson spoke passionately about "the generalist nature of the people who call themselves curricularists." Generalists, Jackson argued, were essential for a vibrant and vital school of education. What is a generalist? Jackson spoke of generalist educators as "scholars in education whose interests are not specifically moored in one of the social science disciplines and who feel they can broadly canvas the wide span of interesting and fascinating issues that make up the field of education in general." In a similar vein, at that same symposium, I heard Elizabeth Vallance put it this way: "Curriculum scholars care about the big picture."

Curriculum studies is particularly amenable to scholars who prefer not to be constrained by a bounded range of ideas, questions, or field-preferred methods of investigation. Curriculum studies is a home for people interested in education broadly and philosophically (What knowledge is of most worth? Who should get what knowledge?). In these ways and more, the field for many a generalist educator fit Jackson well, and it became his field—at least for a while, at least partially.

Jackson's credentials as a curriculum scholar are substantial. He was elected vice president of division B (Curriculum Studies) of AERA for the 1983–1984 term. He was the editor for the AERA-sponsored *Handbook of Research on Curriculum* (Jackson, 1992c). In 1995 he received the division B (Curriculum Studies) Lifetime Achievement Award. I offer these curriculum-specific credentials (his broad list of honors and awards would run for pages) because curriculum studies might not come to mind immediately if educators were asked to identify Jackson's area of scholarship.

THE HIDDEN CURRICULUM

The beginning of Jackson's involvement with curriculum studies is visible, at least in hindsight, in the opening chapter of *Life in Classrooms* (1968). In that chapter, titled "The Daily Grind," Jackson made an early and significant mark on the field: he coined the phrase "the hidden curriculum" (p. 33). The hidden curriculum includes those things students need to learn to be successful in school that are outside of or beyond the expectations of the "official," academic, curriculum.

The hidden curriculum, as Jackson wrote about it in 1968, was largely psychological. It was built from the classroom features of crowds, praise, and power that, Jackson argued, created demands on students and teachers alike. Jackson's hidden curriculum was associated with classroom rewards and punishments, pain and discomfort, and successes and failures, sometimes related to and at other times independent of academic accomplishments.

Although Jackson wrote about the hidden curriculum through the lens of an educational psychologist, soon the idea took hold with curriculum scholars, educational sociologists, and others. For a time there was almost a cottage industry of writing about the hidden curriculum. (For a list of key references, see Jackson, 1992c, p. 9.)

The phrase *the hidden curriculum* was new in 1968, at least as best as I can tell from references in various curriculum sources. Certainly the substantial attention the concept would soon receive was new. But the general idea of the less visible and/or less desirable was embedded in curriculum studies from the start of the field, as Jackson himself would point out a quarter of a century after *Life in Classrooms* in his opening chapter, "Conceptions of Curriculum and Curriculum Specialists," in the *Handbook of Research on Curriculum* (1992c).

As Jackson has explained so well, John Dewey and Franklin Bobbitt, among others, noted that education was not only purposeful but also inadvertent, and not only explicit but also implicit in its dynamics. Dewey wrote about "incidental learning," offering a positive outlook on unplanned but enduring changes of great importance. Bobbitt, generally acknowledged as the author of the first book with the word *curriculum* in its title, took casual note of the undirected experiences that form part of students' education without attending much to the positive or negative consequences of those experiences and without acknowledging the place of undirected experience within the school setting. There is much to be learned from early curriculum writings about what has variously been called incidental learning, undirected as well as directed learning, and inadvertent, unnoticed, or even undesirable learning. But for some reason curriculum scholars (and others) took special note of this phenomenon once Jackson gave it the name "the hidden curriculum."

LEARNING AND TEACHING CURRICULUM HISTORY

If the concept of the hidden curriculum had been Jackson's principal contribution to this field of study, he would, to this day, have a place in the curriculum studies literature. But this was just the start of Jackson's contributions. Increasingly, Jackson began to focus on the "official" curriculum as well, and on the shape and history of curriculum as a field of study.

One significant moment in Jackson's involvement with curriculum studies came with an invitation he received to contribute to the 75th anniversary issue of *The Elementary School Journal* in 1975. Jackson was given a set of articles published in the journal in past years, and from this set he chose to focus on two articles by Franklin Bobbitt. Although Bobbitt was known earlier in his career principally for his contributions to educational administration, the two articles from *The Elementary School Journal* reflected Bobbitt's own transformation from professor of administration to professor of curriculum.

Jackson began a limited study of Bobbitt's work: "My original intention was to confine my reading of Bobbitt to the two reprinted articles, leaving for some later date a closer examination of his many other writings" (1975,

p. 121). But as many of us know to be his custom, Jackson soon found himself more fully steeped in Bobbitt's work. In "Shifting Visions of the Curriculum: Notes on the Aging of Franklin Bobbitt," Jackson (1975) told a story of important developments in the history of curriculum work and a story that offered a critique of the (then) contemporary education conversation.

Jackson's interpretation of Bobbitt's work, work that had been most influential in the early 1900s, was an eerily familiar story of curriculum reform. According to Jackson, Bobbitt railed against the curriculum of the time for its lack of relatedness: to the world outside the classroom, to the nature of the children being taught, and to consideration of the future toward which individual children were headed. Bobbitt argued that educational goals should be rooted in the human abilities to be developed—"what students . . . should be able to do, rather than on what they should know" (1975, p. 124). Bobbitt also argued that specific educational objectives should be derived from and particularized to human activities: health activity, citizenship activity, language activities, leisure occupations, and so on. For this we needed what Bobbitt called "activity analysis." Jackson described activity analysis this way: "Bobbitt's method for making large educational goals digestible is to cut them up into bite-sized chunks!" (p. 125). Finally, Bobbitt argued that education should be individualized for students by their teachers.

Jackson reports briefly on the years of work Bobbitt did with his graduate students at the University of Chicago, addressing his new vision in action. But then Jackson continues the story of Bobbitt's ideas to an unexpected conclusion. Jackson looks further, to the last and longest of Bobbitt's full-length works, published about two decades after *The Elementary School Journal* articles. And it is here that Jackson uncovers a disheartened educator. Jackson writes that Bobbitt seems so much less confident, and so much more doubting and confused.

In contrast to the Bobbitt who began his work in curriculum with great enthusiasm for his new view of education, Jackson found a man at the end of his academic career discouraged about the direction he had taken and the future for such efforts. This attitude seemed all the more important to Jackson because the (then) contemporary conversation about curriculum seemed so much an echo of Bobbitt's work. Jackson examines the change over time in Bobbitt's thinking and looks for lessons therein for contemporary educators.

There is a part of me, I admit, that wants to use this story of Bobbitt's development as a warning to those who seem to have followed in his earlier footsteps. I want to say to them: "See, here is the intellectual grandfather of the movement that has spawned behavioral objectives, Performance Based Teacher Education, and all the rest of such pseudoscientific drivel. Listen to him recanting on his deathbed! All would-be educational engineers take heed and learn your lesson before it is too late!" (1975, p. 132)

Ultimately, Jackson concludes that there is more to the story than simply, and perhaps wrongly, jumping to this conclusion (a conclusion to which I, personally, would like to jump). And so it is with Jackson: He refuses to allow himself or others to settle for quick or easy resolutions for complex issues.

In this respect, reading Jackson is often discomforting. His work is far too considered to allow a reader to walk away carrying a banner for one theme or another. Jackson writes about Bobbitt: "His gift to us . . . may well lie more in his struggle to achieve a vision than in the particular vision he achieved" (1975, p. 132). I feel similarly sometimes about reading Jackson's work. His gift to us may well lie more in his struggle to achieve an understanding of ideas and practices than in advocacy for any the particular ideas and practices. His gift to those of us studying curriculum, perhaps, is to set us on edge, to leave us simultaneously much more knowledgeable and much more uncertain.

THE EXPLICIT/FORMAL CURRICULUM

Following his foray into the work of Franklin Bobbitt, Jackson wrote a variety of articles on curriculum and curriculum studies, with increasing attention to the formal, or explicit, curriculum. My personal favorite among these is "The Reform of Science Education: A Cautionary Tale" (Jackson, 1983). This essay reports on work that took place many years in the past now, and yet the essay hardly reads as dated. It is an incisive and elegant story of an important moment in education in our country that seems to be repeated too often with only minor changes. It is a story of curriculum development, of federal involvement in a system of local school control, of efforts at education change. It is a story of teacher preparation and a story of student achievement. Is there a more current story that could be told?

In at least two small ways "The Reform of Science Education" harkens back to *Life in Classrooms*. First, as Jackson became especially noted for in *Life in Classrooms*, here again he demonstrates the value he places on using all the ways of knowing available to examine questions of significance. Second, as in *Life in Classrooms*, Jackson speaks clearly as a scholar and, simultaneously, as someone intimately connected with active classrooms and practicing teachers.

The "method" to Jackson's work, here and in so many of his publications, does not follow a single orientation to inquiry. Instead, the method is a matter of identifying and examining a problem, turning it upside down and inside out, looking with every lens available, taking advantage of all the tools and techniques and data at his disposal, in search of understanding and explanation. Jackson grabs a question like a bulldog might grab a man's pants leg, holding on and shaking until the question gives in to his relentless tugging.

"The Reform of Science Education" is Jackson's "stock-taking" of the education change movement—principally but not exclusively the science education movement—that took place from, roughly, the 1950s through the 1970s. Jackson begins by generally outlining the history of federal government involvement in American education and curriculum reform, calling attention to the simultaneous (but not balanced) efforts in the directions of equity and excellence. He then traces the growth and direction of the science education movement from its beginning, which, he explains, was well before its popular reference point with the launch of Sputnik.

The sources Jackson calls on are numerous for this relatively short (24-page) article. He reports, for example, on the dollars the National Science Foundation (NSF) invested in curriculum development beginning in 1954 and extending through 1975. As appears to be his habit, he provides context for his numbers by comparing those dollars with various related expenditures. He continues, examining the impact of the dollar investments by considering various NSF studies (a national survey and a set of case studies of teaching practices), National Assessment of Educational Progress (NAEP) reports, meta-analyses of smaller comparative studies, and studies of the secondary effects of the curriculum reform movement.

Jackson provides a good news/bad news picture of the reform movement, taking care to describe and interpret with subtlety rather than with the sledge hammer we are so used to in more public relations–oriented reports. We learn a great deal in this article about the infusion of the federally sponsored materials into schools, including information both about formal adoption and about how materials seem to have been used in classrooms. We learn about change over time in the use of the materials and the federal support for them. Jackson straightforwardly faces the controversies surrounding the materials and the movement in general.

Jackson tackles in detail many of the hows and whys of "things [that] did not work out as planned" (1983, p. 152). He considers explanations that focus on classrooms (including attention to teaching, learning, and learning to teach), explanations that look to curricular decision making (including textbook adoptions) that typically takes place outside of classrooms at the district and state levels of education practice, and explanations associated with tensions with federal curriculum development in a national system of local school control. He summarizes the then-dominant responses to the question of "Where do we go from here?" (p. 156) and continues on to provide his own distinctive answer.

In the end, Jackson wonders aloud about why our concerns about curriculum tend to fixate on one subject or another. He argues instead for attention to the whole of the school curriculum rather than the pieces, and for the collaboration of all who share a common concern for quality:

> All who care deeply about the sorry state of science and math instruction in our schools should be encouraged to join forces with those who care as deeply about other subjects and how well they are taught. . . . One and all must realize that *good* science teachers have more in common with, say, *good* English teachers, and vice versa, than either does with mediocre or poor teachers within their own specialties. . . . The primary loyalty of everyone connected with our schools needs to be to the *quality* of the educational service being provided, rather than to this or that portion of the curriculum, or to this or that institutional role. (1983, pp. 161–162; emphasis in original)

Jackson never created a movement for such a partnership. And it is not clear that he could have if he had wanted to. But one cannot help but wonder if the time will ever come when the whole of the curriculum is treated with as much attention as the various individual school subjects.

CURRICULUM HERE, THERE, AND EVERYWHERE

Jackson's focus on school subjects included attention not only to science but also, especially, to art (Jackson, 1987, 1994). More typically, though, Jackson's work with the formal curriculum has not been subject-centered. Instead, it has focused generally on questions that Kliebard (1979), in particular, has made well known: What should the schools teach (and why should they teach X rather than Y)? Who should get what knowledge? What rules should govern the teaching of the selected subject matter? How should we balance and integrate the various components of the curriculum? With a general orientation toward these questions, it turns out that curriculum issues are almost *everywhere* if you are inclined to see the world that way.

So, for example, in Jackson's curriculum courses at the University of Chicago we read Comenius, Pestalozzi, Froebel, and Rousseau, among others. Of course, these authors have much more to offer than conversation about curriculum. And I suspect that these authors are encountered much more often outside of curriculum classes than inside them. Many areas of education study that would typically fall outside of curriculum studies found their way into curriculum classes Jackson taught. But it was like Jackson to see things differently, to define interesting reading in ways that many of the rest of us might not understand at first and, especially, to weave conversations about curriculum into and around larger conversations about education and schooling.

A class with Phil Jackson was always an adventure. We traveled unexpected routes in our reading about what knowledge is of most worth and who should get what knowledge. We were introduced to scholars from long ago and to contemporary scholars from across the country who came to class and tried out on us their newest ideas. We worked harder than we ever imagined we could or would. It was intense, exciting, and sometimes scary. Eventually, when we left school, we had a rich acquaintance with education ideas spanning time and place and parentage. We would never again think simply or narrowly.

Many of Jackson's publications during this quarter of a century (from, say, 1968 to 1992) were seriously attentive to curriculum issues even when not focused on curriculum per se. In this category I include the stunning triptych of studies of secondary schools published in *Daedalus* in 1981. For this set of articles, on the invitation of *Daedalus* and the schools involved, Jackson visited an inner-city secondary school in Atlanta, a suburban high school outside of Chicago, and a private secondary school in New England. Jackson prepared a separate essay for each school. (Sara Lawrence Lightfoot did the same, for the same schools, in the same issue of the journal.) Jackson's account of each school is full, vivid, and compelling. And while the story Jackson tells about each school involves much more than the school curriculum, curriculum has a significant place in each essay.

In his study of George Washington Carver Comprehensive High School, an urban vocational school, Jackson (1981a) grapples with the curriculum of vocational education. The picture he paints of Carver, a school widely spoken of at that time as successful in its particular mission, is not pretty. Jackson reminds us how easy it is to be patronizing or cynical about education for students in urban schools like this one, and how wrongheaded it would be to take either posture. He asks us to consider "whether and in what terms it is defensible to design and operate at public expense special schools for children of the poor" (p. 54). He nudges us to remember that the practice of vocational education is widespread and yet without the serious attention today that it surely demands for the sake of the students in these programs and the society these students will be participants in for years to come.

In his study of Highland Park High School, a large suburban comprehensive secondary school, Jackson (1981b) examines a curriculum with "something for everyone" (p. 82). He marvels at the diversity of the program offered to the 2,400 students and struggles with the limits to this diversity. Jackson's presentation provides a concrete and moving illustration of what is generally referred to as "scope and sequence" and the consequences for students when they are expected to make their own choices and when early choices have growing consequences. Most especially, Jackson highlights the values that come into play for all curriculum decisions, the possibilities for changes in

er time and in different school contexts, the sources for changes in
d the effects of values on curriculum that have taken place in our
....

In his study of St. Paul's School, a New England boarding school, Jackson (1981c) calls attention to a curriculum that he judges "much more demanding and much more traditional than most public high schools" (p. 122). Jackson finds the St. Paul's curriculum aimed toward preparing students

> to become intelligent and discriminating consumers of, and possibly someday contributors to, the very best our culture has to offer in ideas, artistic achievements, and all the rest. In short, they are being prepared to become the true inheritors of the legacy of humankind's intellectual riches. (p. 124)

Jackson invites us to think about why this curriculum should be reserved for the privileged few, rather than serving as a curriculum for all. He walks us through the various arguments for secondary school curricula that offer more choice to students and curricula that aim at more marketable or vocational skills narrowly defined, and, with great force, he rejects them all.

At first glance, Jackson's call for taking seriously the lessons St. Paul's School offers for all secondary education sounds out of touch with contemporary society, perhaps even undemocratic. But a group of students in a freshman seminar taught me about the deeper power of his argument: the power to engage, provoke, and create a sense of wonder. That is the story I will turn to next.

ENGAGING, PROVOKING, CREATING A SENSE OF WONDER

Two years ago, I assigned two of the three *Daedalus* essays—the stories of Carver, the urban vocational school, and St. Paul's, the New England boarding school—to students in a freshman seminar at San José State University. The title of the seminar was "Public Education and its Discontents." Our aim during the semester was to examine access to education, ideas about excellence in education, and public attitudes toward education over the course of the 20th century.

It took us a while to get to the Jackson articles. We began with *A Nation at Risk* (National Commission on Excellence in Education, 1983), which was published at just about the time the students in this class were born. The whole of the students' educational experiences was shaped at least in some ways by this report. The students were moderately interested. We read some Lawrence Cremin (from *Popular Education and Its Discontents*), some Patricia Graham ("What America Has Expected of Its Schools over the

Past Century"), some David Berliner and Bruce Biddle (from *The Manufactured Crisis*), some Jeannie Oakes (from *Keeping Track*). We collected statistics and studied legal decisions and federal legislation. Class session after class session, the students remained moderately interested and involved. None of our work appealed to all of the students; each of the students showed interest in some of what we were reading and discussing. The students were not turned off to our studies, but neither were they turned on—until we arrived at the Jackson essays.

Suddenly the students came alive. They attended carefully to details in the essays, arguing with one another about exactly what Jackson had written and what he intended to convey. Talk among the students about aspects of the essays began before the official start of the class and continued after the metaphorical bell signaled the class end. One student brought the web address for St. Paul's School to our class and shared a wealth of new information about the school. While my presence in class and my questions were helpful (I hope!), these essays were teachers in their own right.

The story of the urban high school, while not the story for any of the students in the class, all of whom had taken college prep classes while in high school, was close enough to their experiences to make them uneasy, uncertain, defensive, and sometimes just plain angry. My students knew others who had had school experiences similar to Jackson's description of life at Carver. They worried about the future for these classmates (and, in two instances, the future for their siblings). They were angry at the adults who seemed so disrespectful of the students. Like Jackson, they were baffled by a curriculum that included 800 hours of schoolwork in "marketable skills" just so students might hold jobs like the ones these students had held or were holding even at the moment with little more than a day or two of training. Yet they were also bothered by the assumption that a high school education should be a requirement for all, that high school was the only (or at least the best) place to learn to do the many things that students uninterested in academic work might prefer to learn. And they seemed uncomfortable that, until they read this essay, they had never given much thought to the difference between their school experiences and the experiences of students in a vocational track.

The story of St. Paul's School was so far outside the experiences of my students that the school could have been located in another country or on a different planet. My students were amazed, stunned, captivated, curious, and just plain confused about this account. They did not seem to wish the St. Paul's experience for themselves; schooling like that at St. Paul's seemed to come with expectations that they did not want to be held to or measured by. They found no appeal in the idea of remaining on school premises day and night, week after week and month after month, no matter how well endowed the setting. They did not want to be *protected* from what Jackson called "various nonschool *mis*educative experiences and influences, such as activities that cut into the time needed for study . . . or the companionship of persons who are not serious about education" (1981c, p. 121). Most thought they would be interested in the curriculum of St. Paul's School, but not if it meant they would have to sacrifice life and learning outside of school. And yet they wondered about their place in the world if others were prepared in ways they were not, both for higher education and for adult responsibilities.

As we discussed the Jackson essays in class, the students seemed deeply engaged, attentive to detail, curious about a line of argument, interested in trying their hand at arguing back, and automatically making meaningful connections to other work we had read earlier in the semester that had elicited much less attention at the time. After two class sessions devoted to the essays, we moved on in our reading and our research. But Jackson's writing continued to be present in our conversations and in the students' writing. At the end of the semester, as the students worked on final papers and exams, it was clear that Jackson had burned a hole in their thinking.

Jackson had engaged these students, provoked them, and left them with a sense of wonder. Of course, it is not just college freshmen who respond this way to Jackson's writing. Jackson pushes us all to think differently, to see more and see more deeply, to ask questions we might never have thought of before, to wonder. After reading Jackson, we know a great deal more than when we began, and yet we also know that there is so much more to learn.

A QUARTER OF A CENTURY OF STUDY

When Jackson was invited to edit the AERA-sponsored *Handbook of Research on Curriculum* (1992c), some curriculum scholars might have been perplexed by the choice. Jackson is much better known for his work on teaching, or on Dewey, than for his work in curriculum studies. He does not stand as a leader of any group of curriculum scholars who have staked out a visible and bounded territory within the curriculum field. To the best of my knowledge, he has never had a "research program" in the field. He appears to have followed his interests wherever they have taken him, and for however long they have carried him, without concern for his place in the curriculum field.

Yet Jackson has moved in and out of the study of curriculum history, theory, and practice, and he has demonstrated a wide-ranging knowledge of the field. He has been attentive to its central thrusts, to emerging lines of work, and to historical contributions that are embedded still (or not) in contemporary conversation. He has considered the scope and collection of work under the curriculum studies label, frequently integrating ideas from curriculum factions and moving past the dualities that sometimes result from a narrower focus.

Jackson's broad perspective and lack of partisanship may well have been important in choosing him to edit the first AERA-sponsored curriculum handbook. Undoubtedly, his perspective and lack of partisanship served him well as he orchestrated the making of the "handbook" that is 1,088 pages long, divided into four parts and 34 chapters. Jackson wrote the opening chapter, "Conceptions of Curriculum and Curriculum Specialists." As you probably already presume, that chapter addresses curriculum writ large, questions related to "the curriculum as a topic of concern in its own right and as a field of professional endeavor" (1992c, p. 3).

With his work on the *Handbook*, and the larger body of attention he has given to curriculum studies over a quarter of a century, we see a continuing way of working as an education scholar—one that brings to life the habits of mind Dewey called attention to in *How We Think* (LW.8). Jackson consistently is open-minded, whole-hearted, and responsible. Dewey wrote this about open-mindedness:

> It includes an active desire to listen to more sides than one; to give heed to facts from whatever source they come; to give full attention to alternative possibilities; to recognize the possibility of error even in the beliefs that are dearest to us. (LW.8.136)

Dewey had this to say about whole-heartedness:

> When a person is absorbed, the subject carries him on. Questions occur to him spontaneously; a flood of suggestions pour in on him; further inquiries and readings are indicated and followed; . . . the material holds and buoys his mind up and gives an onward impetus to thinking. (LW.8.137)

And Dewey explained responsibility like this:

> To be intellectually responsible is to consider the consequences of a projected step; it means to be willing to adopt these consequences when they follow reasonably from any position already taken. Intellectual responsibility secures integrity; that is to say, consistency and harmony in belief. (LW.8.138)

In sum, Dewey described Jackson's way of working.

And yet this is not the whole story. Jackson not only has been open-minded, whole-hearted, and responsible; he has also been insightful and elegant in his continuing, if intermittent, work in curriculum studies. Whether he has focused on the subject matters, or the distribution of knowledge, or the principles guiding decisions about what knowledge is of most worth or how that knowledge should be shared, he invariably engages us, provokes us, and leaves us with a sense of wonder. Reading Jackson—on teaching, on schooling, on curriculum, or on virtually any topic he has examined—changes how we think.

The Misunderstood Curriculum

Karen Zumwalt

JUDD HALL was the center of my life for 4 years from 1969 to 1973. And in true Chicago fashion, it was another five years—3 years teaching at Smith College and 2 years at Teachers College—before I was finally awarded that increasingly rare and now extinct degree, a Ph.D. in education from the University of Chicago.

In the late 1960s, the conflict between generations, the civil rights movement, the Vietnam War, and the emerging feminist movement rocked the nation. And in Chicago, the Democratic Convention in 1968 and the student protests that shook the university in 1969 brought the turmoil of the era to the Midway. It was a scary time and an exhilarating time; our generation was going to change the world. Educational institutions were seen as both a target of change and an instrument of change.

It was the fall of 1969, when things had calmed down a little, that five or six of us entered the doctoral program in Curriculum and Philosophy. Many of us had 3-year full scholarships and stipends thanks to the National Defense Education Act. Although I wasn't aware of it at the time, that NDEA support was one of the defining features of my doctoral studies. Unlike many of our doctoral students today who are forced to study part-time and, if lucky, take a 1-semester or 1-year sabbatical for full-time studies, we had the luxury of gathering in Judd Hall for mid-morning coffee with other students and professors. Although Dewey and Tyler were long gone, it was a star-studded faculty—I remember Phil Jackson, of course, Joe Schwab, Dan Lortie, Benjamin Bloom, Ian Westbury, Robert Dreeben, Jack Getzels, Kevin Ryan, Herb Thelan, Fred Lighthall, Bruno Bettleheim, among others, and the first woman who gained tenure in the social sciences division in a very long time, Susan Stodolosky. As I picture those heady discussions in Judd Hall, I have clear memories of sitting at the feet of Schwab and lengthy conversations with Westbury. Despite the headline events of the late 1960s and early 1970s, the big, consuming question we kept returning to was: What is curriculum? Navel-gazing perhaps, but Schwab's (1969) *School Review* article declaring the field of curriculum moribund appeared in our first quarter at Chicago.

My two other advisers were less frequently there, not having the luxury of a morning coffee break—Stodolosky being the new mother of twins and Jackson being the director of the University of Chicago Lab School. For me, their unique positions were another defining factor in shaping the decisions I was to make throughout my career.

More specifically, a new course, co-taught by Jackson and Stodolosky, "Education 395: Teachers and Children in Classrooms," developed into my dissertation, a year-long observational study of 25 seventh graders in the Lab School. And although Susan was clearly in psychology and Phil was just in the early stages of his metamorphosis from psychology to curriculum (and, later, to philosophy), what I learned from them also shaped my understanding of the "what is curriculum" question that consumed us doctoral students in curriculum at the time. Phil's *Life in Classrooms* (1968), which made the hidden curriculum come alive, had just been published. Susan was questioning experimental and correlational research that did not look inside the "black box"—or what was actually happening in the classroom. Her insistence that the "treatment" could not be assumed to have been carried out in the same way and her call for looking at unplanned outcomes as well as what was intended seems commonsensical now, but it wasn't at the time. So here were two psychologists talking about the curriculum—the hidden curriculum and curriculum in action—which we were grappling with as doctoral students in Curriculum and Philosophy.

Once you get this Chicago way of thinking about curriculum, it is hard to think of curriculum in any other way. So when René Arcilla, Mary Driscoll, and David Hansen invited us to listen to our instincts and to use this opportunity to think aloud about teaching and education, I kept coming back to what I had learned from Phil and others at Chicago and my continual frustration with the popular use of the word *curriculum*—a course of study. (Interestingly, using its Latin derivation, "a racecourse" might be a more apt description, given today's high school students racing to fit as many AP courses into their schedule as possible.)

But this seemed too simple a notion. Yet if it was so simple, why does it seem so elusive? Then I reread the letter inviting us "to speak about an aspect of teaching and education that you love, in the educational spirit evoked in Wordsworth's autobiographical poem where he says to us: 'What we have loved/Others will love/ And we may show them how.'" While more lofty than my aspirations, it does provide a rationale for what I have chosen to explore in this essay. It also relates specifically to my own conception of a curricular vision of teaching for which I am indebted to Phil and others at the University of Chicago (Darling-Hammond et al., 2005; Snyder, Bolin, & Zumwalt, 1992; Zumwalt, 1989).

To follow Wordsworth's cues, I first share with you why I think the "what is curriculum" question is more than just a frame for an interesting semantic debate among graduate students and their professors. I do this by using some examples of how the traditional conception of curriculum has affected the enactment of the new citywide public school curriculum in New York City. To illustrate a fuller, more powerful, but elusive conception of curriculum, in Jacksonian tradition, I turn to thinking about a familiar phenomena, the college curriculum. I then return to how this enriched sense of curriculum has practical implications for teachers facing unidimensional visions of curriculum in this age of accountability. In conclusion, I hope that I will have led you to a curricular vision of teaching as an appropriate image for teaching in the 21st century.

CURRICULUM IN NEW YORK CITY TODAY

These days in New York City, "the curriculum" is the punishment given to schools that are not successful enough, according to politically adjusted criteria, to get a waiver from the mandated curriculum. After adjustments were made, initially 208 schools were exempted from "the curriculum." Despite the fact that the newly mandated reading and math curriculum is not based on highly structured, skills-based approaches to reading and math, schools scrambled to be declared exempt from the "progressive approaches" that many of them have embraced for years and continue to practice.

Obviously, to obtain a waiver was a badge of honor, but beyond that school people knew that a mandated curriculum often leads to rules and checklists regardless of the nature of the curriculum. Hence, the "rocking chair" rule for reading areas pops up as administrators push teachers to adhere to certain program components. While school officials deny they are requiring certain furnishings, this is how some administrators interpreted the principle of designing classroom spaces that are conducive to reading and deep discussion.

Some misinterpretations come from a lack of understanding of the conception of teaching and learning implicit in New York City's new mandated curriculum by administrators and teachers who are used to implementing curriculum handed down by the district. As the new mandated curriculum was being implemented, one of my doctoral students fed me weekly examples from her consulting work with math and literacy coaches in city schools. There is the teacher, eager to show that she meets the new guidelines of providing children's literature to match children's reading levels, who has neatly labeled her new library of children's books as "above average," "average," and "below average." One day my student had spent the day observing math in one school and had made notes about possible areas of discussion with the teachers. Much to her surprise and disgust, the next day her list of starting points for discussion had been translated into a checklist to evaluate teachers! Perhaps it is not surprising that the new curriculum is being so misunderstood because it not only incorporates a different understanding of teaching and learning, but it runs counter to the traditional conception of curriculum as something to be implemented rather than something to be adapted and enacted by empowered teachers.

That the traditional notion of curriculum is deeply embedded in the system became even clearer to me, right after the new citywide curriculum was adopted, when the Board of Education's Institutional Review Board began rejecting students' doctoral dissertation proposals. One of our top students, who was involved in a new teacher induction program, was interested in studying how new teachers become curriculum makers within the current testing context. Initially, she was told her proposal could not be approved because there was no purpose in studying curriculum since next year, when she would be collecting data, all the teachers would be using the same curriculum and there was no room for them "to play with it." They were even thinking of having a moratorium on any research on curriculum. After many long e-mails and phone conversations, she was able to convince the person she was talking to that curriculum enactment was not a subversive activity. He thought he could get it accepted if she took the words *teacher as curriculum maker* out of the title. Although things seemed to have gotten better with the review panel, another student recently had trouble getting approval for her proposal on how third-grade teachers in heterogeneous classes differentiate curriculum to meet the needs of their diverse learners. Instead of using the highly acceptable term *differentiated instruction*, she had purposely used *differentiated curriculum* because she wanted to capture a more holistic approach to differentiation that included broader aspects of the teaching and learning context, such as content, interactions among class members, the physical setting, grouping arrangements, and class climate. She wanted to study the *differentiated curriculum*, not just instruction. After submitting multiple explanations of what she meant by the enacted curriculum, she finally was given approval.

While it is probably unrealistic to expect that the word *curriculum* will ever be used differently by New York City's officials, Phil's work motivates me to help people see beyond the everyday uses—to see the power of a multidimensional vision of something that seems so straightforward and simple. Before exploring the power of a different vision of curriculum than is pervasive not just in New York City but in a nation enamored with a corporate model of accountability as the way to fix the public schools, I need to elaborate the many dimensions of "curriculum" that bring this concept alive in a way that makes connections for the reader with familiar, memorable experiences.

A BROADER CONCEPTION OF CURRICULUM

To illustrate a broader conception of curriculum, I played with a couple of ideas. I could develop examples drawn from in Eliot Eisner's (1995) monograph *The Hidden Consequences of a National Curriculum*. They were sufficiently generic examples to help policymakers understand the power of an enriched sense of curriculum, but I decided they were too simplistic for this purpose (Zumwalt, 1995). I could use examples from a presentation I had done for my local high school PTA a couple of years ago. Some parents had heard my references to the hidden curriculum in opposing the board's move of the fifth grade to the middle school and had asked me to talk about the hidden curriculum of the high school. I based my analysis on a year's worth of student newspapers and my experiences as a parent of two high school students. While informative for the parents and fun for me, the examples were too situated in local context for this purpose.

Writing for an academic audience, I could use Teachers College as an example, but I decided that might be a little too provocative and risky. The conference honoring Phil was fast approaching when the answer came to me in the middle of my son's Parents' Weekend. Reflecting on *Life in Classrooms* (1968), I remembered the power of reading about everyday classroom events seen through a different lens. Using the familiar to illustrate the complexities of a deceptively simple concept was a powerful technique that Phil taught us. Right in front of me was some curriculum thinking I had been doing for the past 2 years as my youngest child applied to and entered college. So with apologies to Georgetown and to Scott for presenting a partial picture based on less than three semesters, I decided to reflect on what I have observed, as a way of illustrating thinking about curriculum in a more holistic way than the term connotes to most people, even those working in educational institutions.

As a parent of a 2003 college graduate and a college sophomore, I had been thinking a lot about college curriculums recently. Two different children; two different curriculums stemming from one majoring in biology at a small public, specialized college associated with a private university and the other studying the social sciences at a Catholic university. Besides the basic trappings of being away from home and living in coed dorms, the main similarity is that both Syracuse and Georgetown are big basketball colleges—and have a long time rivalry. Now that's a whole topic in itself—the impact of college sports on the college curriculum.

But let me stay focused on illustrating the concept of curriculum using my son's experience. Georgetown has a distinctive curriculum for students in the liberal arts college. Besides the usual liberal arts distribution requirements, all students must take one course in philosophy, one in ethics, and two in theology. Except for one course in theology called "The Problem of God," all other requirements involve a multitude of choices. Actually "The Problem of God" course had 23 different sections offering quite different approaches to the "same" content—something that Joe Schwab would have really appreciated.

Hence, the actual course of study taken by students meeting the general curriculum requirements is different. Add 33 majors, 44 minors, 8 certificate fields, and more than 90 study-abroad sites, used by 50% of the undergraduates, and one can see that very few undergraduates have the same course of study. However, the *formal or explicit curriculum* requirements place parameters and shape the curriculum in very different ways than at other colleges. It is usually at this level of curriculum that prospective students and parents are attracted or not attracted to certain colleges.

A few prospective students go further than looking at the catalogue of courses and, thanks to the Internet, can actually look at the syllabi of current courses—the closest view most students get to the *planned or intended curriculum* before choosing their courses. But savvy students figure out very soon that even when there is an agreed-upon curriculum syllabus, the *enacted curriculum* can be very different depending on who is teaching it and which students are taking the course that semester.

As my son started choosing his courses the summer before his freshman year, I noticed he was picking sections based on the time of day. He wanted to sleep as late as possible. I suggested he also look at the student course evaluations that were posted by the student newspaper. He did, and I did the same. Interestingly, we came up with different choices. I found out that while I was looking at the student satisfaction rating, he was looking at the rating indicating how much work was involved. He finally accepted my argument that the satisfaction rating was more important, because if a course were really too much work, the professor would not have a high rating. He is still thanking me for getting him into the best "Calculus 2" section. And after choosing to build his courses around an "awesome" sociology professor his sophomore year, he has decided that the professor is far more important than the time of day.

He did decide, however, when choosing his "Problem of God" section, that time of the day and rating/reputation of the professor were not as important as content. Not having had any formal religious education, he was less than enthusiastic about most of the choices and a little scared about not having the background of most of the students. There was only one section he wanted—one focused on 9/11 and two questions: Does organized religion inherently lead to violence? And when, if ever, is it appropriate to call someone "evil"? As a New Yorker whose senior year in high school will always be framed by that tragic event, he felt a deep connection to the way the professor had framed the content and some confidence that he could bring something to the course. He put it as his first priority and, fortunately, got into the course. So professor, content, and other students who might be taking the course all influenced his course selection because he had quickly learned the importance of the enacted curriculum.

And then there is what Jackson (1968) has called the *hidden curriculum*—the lessons students learn that are not necessarily part of the planned or even the enacted curriculum, although they may be an integral part of both, either intentionally or unintentionally. The hidden curriculum involves learned outcomes that are not openly acknowledged to the learners and sometimes not even known by the teacher. Once the teacher explicitly acknowledges the outcomes or once the learners are aware of them, the lessons are no longer part of the hidden curriculum (Martin, 1976).

Most of the questions on the college tours my son took at Georgetown were from parents and prospective students trying to figure out how Catholic the college really is. Georgetown, founded by John Carroll in 1789 to be religiously pluralistic, is clearly and proudly a Catholic institution in the Jesuit tradition, but approximately half the students today are non-Catholic. The questions indicated people were wondering about the hidden curriculum: Did it subtly restrict how professors taught their classes or how student life in the dorms was controlled? While the Catholic hierarchy might wonder whether Georgetown is Catholic enough, these parents and students were trying to figure out whether it really was as inclusive as the college claimed to be. On the weekend for accepted students, the clearest indication that the hidden curriculum did not contradict the professed inclusiveness and open expression was the 10-foot student-hung banner over the archway of "Red Square"—which everyone had to pass through several times—congratulating accepted gay, lesbian, and bisexual students. It remained up the entire weekend.

Another example that struck me was the pride the college's rabbi had in announcing that in the past decade, more Georgetown graduates had become rabbis than Brandeis graduates. My Jewish friends tell me that this may say more about Brandeis than Georgetown, but I still think it is an intriguing fact and wonder whether it might be the consequence of a selection factor relating to the core curriculum requirements, the enacted curriculum, or the hidden curriculum for Jewish students finding themselves at a Jesuit college.

By the way, either accidentally or by intentionally capitalizing on students' radar for "gut" courses, one of the more popular courses at the college is one on Israeli culture, thus introducing students to content and perspectives that they might not have been likely to choose. This raises another aspect of the hidden curriculum that is created by the peer culture. While the impact of the peer culture could be another essay in itself, let me just illustrate by using an example given by an assistant dean at Parents' Weekend as he talked to sophomores and their parents about choosing majors and minors. When students come to talk to him about their indecision, he reminds them that "the current carries dead bodies downstream." The current—or, in our terms, the hidden curriculum—is strong pressures from the student culture—double majoring and studying abroad for résumé building, choosing certain majors to position one best for professional schools, and majoring in government or economics because you, too, might follow illustrious alumni into important government positions . . . maybe even the presidency. By making them aware of this aspect of the hidden curriculum, he was hoping that by making it visible it might not hold such a sway on their own decision making.

And then there is the *experienced* curriculum. Even if there were another student in all the same courses and in the same dormitories as my son, there is no one who experiences the curriculum the way he does. He experiences the enacted and hidden curriculum differently because of his personality, gender, race, socioeconomic background, affluent public school experience, suburban New York childhood, and membership in a religious minority.

And the curriculum he experiences is different because he has made some choices about his noncourse experiences. He had an "aha!" experience at one of the voluntary freshmen retreats, appropriately called ESCAPE, offered by the campus ministry. He realized he didn't come to Georgetown to have the dorm experience. He could have that anywhere; he came to take advantage of Washington, D.C. After that ESCAPE weekend, he intentionally made Washington part of his college curriculum by getting a part-time internship with his congresswoman the next year and by exploring the city—its museums, events at embassies, and the numerous political speakers and events that are offered at Georgetown. His leadership role in the College Democrats is teaching him competencies and skills he could not gain in a college class. This is the curriculum he has created and is creating for himself.

A CURRICULAR VISION OF TEACHING IN
THE AGE OF ACCOUNTABILITY

Thinking of curriculum in all its manifestations—the explicit, planned, enacted, hidden, and experienced curriculum—provides a much fuller and powerful conception that makes it impossible to think of "curriculum" in the commonly used one-dimensional manner that might be captured in a few descriptive paragraphs in a college catalogue or in a district mandate. It also makes it impossible to think of teaching as something separate from curriculum. They are intertwined. It is this curricular vision of teaching that can give hope to teachers who are increasingly discouraged about teaching in the current political context that emphasizes accountability in terms of standardized test scores (Costigan & Crocco, 2004).

As a teacher educator, helping my graduate students develop a critical perspective about the current educational scene is relatively easy; helping them cope with the phenomena on a daily basis, however, is more difficult. The three facts of classroom life that Jackson spoke about—praise, crowds, power—are still "three facets of life with which even the youngest student must learn to deal" (p. 10), but they have been dramatically shaped by the No Child Left Behind (NCLB) legislation that has changed the explicit, planned, enacted, hidden, and experienced curriculum, particularly at the elementary school level (Starnes, 2006).

In this NCLB era, there are some lines from Jackson's 1968 text that stand out in striking contrast to the situation in many elementary schools today. In talking about the evaluative environment of classrooms, Jackson comments, "In the lower grades formal tests are almost nonexistent, although evaluation clearly occurs" (pp. 19–20). He talks of how schools are "reward-oriented," stressing "the pedagogical advantages of success and the disadvantages of failure" (p. 25). He talks of elementary teachers being more "activity oriented" than learning oriented, focusing on involvement rather than outcomes (p. 162). Basically, the "praise" facet has taken on a more formal dimension in this era of NCLB accountability with its high-stakes testing. Scrutiny of students' strengths and weakness is even more public than Jackson describes. The "power" even elementary students must cope with is not only the authority of the classroom teacher but also the power of government-mandated tests that determine an individual pupil's success and failure—the provision of remedial services, promotion to the next grade, and, ultimately, graduation from high school—and consume the life of schools (Lewis, 2006; Winerip, 2006). Based on standardized test scores, whole schools, not just individual students, can be labeled as failing. Hence, there is tremendous pressure on teachers to orient their work toward making sure that their students do well (or even better) on achievement tests. The result has been that test preparation and "teaching to the tests" have driven the curriculum, even in schools that should have no fear of failing. Schools have responded by increasing the time dedicated to reading and math, while minimizing or even eliminating recess, music, art, social studies, and science (Starnes, 2006). In some schools, the planned curriculum has been replaced with a publishing company's scripted lessons based on "scientific" evidence that test score gains will result. In extreme cases, administrators check that there is no deviation so that the planned and enacted curricula are synonymous. We seem to be in the midst of an extreme manifestation of what Jackson called the "engineering " approach to education (1968, p. 166).

In too many schools, it is very troubling to see teaching reduced to the technical task of following a scripted "curriculum" and measured solely by test scores. Proliferation of this vision of teaching has the potential to chase good teachers, as well as students, away from schools. One of the attractions of public school teaching has been that even beginners are allowed a level of autonomy and creativity not available in many other entry-level jobs. Teaching as I have experienced it, directly and indirectly through my undergraduate and graduate students, "has been intellectually and emotionally challenging, calling on one's knowledge, life experiences, creativity, organizational skills and personal sensitivities" (Zumwalt, 2004, p. 25). In too many schools, this is not what teaching has become.

While outright rebellion or leaving teaching might seem like the only alternatives in some cases, teachers need other ways to think about life in classroom and schools that sustain them and their students. The public does have a right to expect that students are meeting expectations and, in the foreseeable future, achievement tests are likely to be a major way that such accountability is assured. This reality needs to be faced by today's teachers, students, parents, administrators, and teacher educators, even as they work to change the domination of this view of schooling.

Most of the prospective and practicing teachers with whom I work have not given up in the face of the current challenges that they feel negatively affect their teaching and the education for their students. In most situations, proactive teachers can find space for themselves and their students to break through in all but the most rigidly prescriptive environments. Often, but not always, they are rewarded for doing so by their students, administrators, and parents whose conceptions of good teaching go beyond improvement in test scores and who realize that the curriculum is a more dynamic concept than what is mandated in any written document.

Central to their continued empowerment as teachers is viewing teaching itself as an act of curriculum making (Darling-Hammond et al., 2005; Snyder et al., 1992; Zumwalt, 1989). Curriculum is something that is created rather than just something to be implemented. Even when the *formal or explicit curriculum* is embodied in a prescriptive *planned curriculum* that looks like a script to be followed, the *curriculum* that gets *enacted* by specific teachers with different groups of children in different contextual settings is and should be different, as teachers respond to the needs of their students. Good teachers also realize that the *curriculum* that is *experienced* by individual students, even in cases of whole-class instruction, is different. They also realize that the consequences of their students' and their own words and actions, organizational and managerial choices made in the classroom and by the administration, and the culture of the school and community create aspects of the curriculum that is *hidden* from the students and sometimes even the teacher.

While their degrees of freedom may be more constrained than in the past and in some settings more than others, teachers who understand their inextricable role in creating curriculum realize the active role they can take in translating the explicit curriculum into the planned curriculum and in transforming the planned curriculum into the enacted curriculum. In terms of the hidden and experienced curriculum, they realize that "the teacher has it within his power to chill some of the abrasive aspects of school life *if he so desires*" (Jackson, 1968, p.154; emphasis in original). With "a dual allegiance—to the preservation of both the institution and the individuals who inhabit it," the teacher recognizes that "the individual student often stands in need of protection of a sort, from those qualities of classroom life that threaten his sense of uniqueness and personal worth" (p. 154).

For example, the teacher might reflect on what the intended and unintended messages students may be receiving in today's classroom, where testing can become such a major part of the explicit, planned, and enacted curriculum. Some may be important lessons from the "crowds, praise, power" phenomena of classroom life that students need to master as they make their way through school. Other lessons may be viewed as constricting and negative. What are the students learning about what is worth knowing, the types of learning and thinking that are valued, and the purposes of schooling? Have they come to see learning as only instrumentally rather than intrinsically valuable? Are they equating test scores with personal worth? What do they see as the relationship among success, luck, effort, ability, and opportunity? What messages are they getting about children like themselves and what society offers them in contrast to what they see in the media or even in other classrooms in the school? In analyzing the possible hidden curriculum as experienced by their students, teachers might decide to counter it with a different hidden curriculum or explicitly make different learnings a part of the planned and enacted curriculum. To do so takes initiative that goes considerably beyond thinking about how to plan and enact the explicit curriculum.

While this kind of reflection and explicit attention to the hidden curriculum may help teachers find a place for their voice within the accountability-driven school environment, Jackson also reminds us that teachers' perspectives may naturally prompt "actions that may serve as antidotes to the toxic qualities of institutional life" (1968, p. 152). He talks about how the humanness of teachers, their feelings of uncertainty and fallibility, and their empathic responses to a student as a person, not just as a role, are ways that "soften the impact of the impersonal institution." When I have asked teachers and even superintendents in a very test-conscious county to describe the best teachers they ever had, the best teachers in their district, or the best teachers their children have, the answers are very similar. Invariably, test scores are not mentioned. Instead, the "best" teachers are described as "having high standards and expectations for students, engaging the students in memorable curriculum activities, and, most frequently, personally connecting to individual students in some meaningful way—making students feel special, confident, able, valued, connected, motivated, or empowered. These are teachers who make a difference in the lives of their students" (Zumwalt, 2004, p. 257).

It is in the classroom that the curriculum, in its many intentional and unintentional manifestations, comes alive—this is where curriculum is given meaning and where the reflective teacher can play a critical, interactive role. Viewing curriculum this way opens up the potential for initiative by teachers that might seem prohibited by prescriptive curriculum mandates. It provides an analytic tool for teachers to deepen their reflective inquiry about curriculum and the basic understanding that teachers cannot help but be part of the curriculum—the learning that students take with them. With such an understanding, teachers gain the opportunity to shape what their students are learning—an opportunity to make a difference despite the constraints of an overly prescriptive explicit curriculum.

It is this curricular vision of teaching that I view as the image of teaching for the 21st century. This is a vision that sees the planning and interactive stages of teaching as places where curriculum is created through decisions about content, instructional strategies, classroom organization and management, teacher and peer interactions; where intended and unintended purposes are considered; where assumptions are not made about how individual students experience the curriculum based on the enacted curriculum; where the curriculum created by the administrators, teachers, and students outside the classroom—as well as what's happening inside the classroom—is acknowledged and deliberated on.

Although he did not use these specific words, this is the living, powerful conception of curriculum that Jackson made so accessible in *Life in Classrooms* (1968)—a book that also represents his own journey from viewing the world through psychological lenses to a broader, interdisciplinary curricular vision. Jackson wrote the book "especially for teachers, administrators and others whose daily work brings them into direct contact with classroom life" (p. vii). Almost 40 years later, it is his way of seeing that still provides hope to teachers who are committed to children "who spend their day in that collection of enclosures" called classrooms.

In Search of the Extraordinary in the Ordinary:Philip Jackson and/on John Dewey

David A. Granger and Craig A. Cunningham

I N THE EARLY 1990s, the two of us were attending an annual Philosophy of Education Society conference, talking with a prominent philosopher of education about our studies with Philip Jackson at the University of Chicago. We mentioned that we were reading and analyzing some of John Dewey's later philosophical works. Our interlocutor expressed genuine surprise: "What does Phil know about Dewey?" he asked, innocently enough. At that point in time, you see, Jackson had not published anything explicitly or specifically on Dewey's philosophy or other writings, save for a brief essay on "John Dewey's Poetry" that had appeared in the *American Journal of Education* in 1982.

Times have certainly changed. We expect that few philosophers of education today remain unaware of Jackson's interest in and expertise on Dewey. Since the early 1990s, he has published a major introduction to the reissue of Dewey's renowned works *The School and Society* and *The Child and the Curriculum* (1990c). Jackson has also published two wide-ranging studies of Dewey's thought: *John Dewey and the Lessons of Art* (1998b) and *John Dewey and the Philosopher's Task* (2002b). These books—in addition to several important articles and (we hope) another book in the works—have established Jackson as one of the foremost commentators on Dewey's philosophy, not just among educators, but in the philosophical community as well.

So what accounts for Jackson's recent public interest in Dewey, especially Dewey's later philosophical works? This essay endeavors to answer that question. We begin by recounting a few biographical details relevant to the origins of Jackson's gradual rediscovery of Dewey in the late 1960s and early 1970s. Following this, we describe some of the ways in which Jackson's writing style reflects Deweyan elements and ideas. Finally, we attempt to identify some of the lessons that Jackson seems to have learned from studying Dewey's later works on metaphysics and aesthetics. It is our hope that this essay not only sheds light on Jackson's interest and expertise in Dewey but also demonstrates how attention to Dewey's philosophy has deepened Jackson's understanding of the purposes and methods of education and of the human condition more generally.

WHY DEWEY?

Jackson was not, as he will readily admit, trained as a philosopher. Rather, he began his career as a psychometrician. Yet as early as the 1950s, as he began his career first at Wayne State University and then at the University of Chicago, Jackson felt unease about the larger significance of his quantitative work and continually sought methods to study the more holistic aspects of human experience. Even his pioneering work with Jacob Getzels developing measures of creativity left Jackson feeling dissatisfied, as if he had been to the feast but somehow ended up at the wrong table. He longed for a better understanding of life's qualitative immediacies, those ultimately ineffable or indescribable aspects of life that represent the difference between merely mechanical behaviors and the sublimely human.

While on sabbatical at the Center for Advanced Study in the Behavioral Sciences at Stanford University in 1962–1963, Jackson had the opportunity to participate in a seminar with a group of anthropologists who were studying primate behavior. He was very much struck by their comments about the different behaviors observed in the wild versus in captivity, and he wondered whether similar differences would exist if young people were observed in their "natural" settings versus being studied through the usual paper-and-pencil tests. His growing unease with the instruments he had been trained to use naturally reinforced his discomfort with the limited range of information that had counted as data. Jackson began to suspect that the qualitative techniques of anthropology and ethnography could be fruitfully applied to the study of the humanistic qualities of educational settings. What is more, the use of new methods of observation had the potential to lead to new insights as well. As Jackson (1990b) tells it in his Introduction to the reissue of *Life in Classrooms*:

> Learning how to see things differently, whether inside classrooms or anywhere else, makes a great deal of difference in how we respond to our surroundings. . . . Waking to a fresh view of things invariably alters the way we think and subsequently act, even though the connections between perception, thought, and action may be greatly attenuated and all but impossible to verify. This is the faith of both art and science, whose insights continually awaken us to an altered vision of the world.
>
> How does this awakening happen? There doubtless are many ways that it occurs but a chief one, if I am to believe what took place during my visits to classrooms, is through enlarging upon the meaning or significance of something we already know. Indeed, on the basis of that experience I would further suggest that the common and ordinary aspects of our lives, to which classrooms certainly belong, are precisely the parts that call most urgently for renewed vision. (p. xviii)

The experience of sitting in classrooms and really paying attention to what he saw there confirmed Jackson's earlier belief that the quantitative methods of the psychometricians were missing crucial information concerning the nature of intelligence, teaching, schooling, and life itself. Indeed, Jackson's eye-opening experiences as he sat in the back of classrooms during the next few years proved not only to open his eyes, but, with the publication of *Life in Classrooms* (1968), to open the entire field of educational research to the possibility that qualitative methods might lead to transformative insights for the improvement of education. Moreover, Jackson came eventually to believe that it is only by escaping the boundaries of what is measurable that researchers can add anything of value that teachers don't already know or could know in their everyday practice.

Around the time *Life in Classrooms* was going to press, Jackson's colleague Harold Dunkel convinced him of the value of reading more deeply in the work of John Dewey. Dunkel thought that Jackson's expanding interest in understanding the qualitative aspects of experience would be rewarded by careful study of Dewey's later works, including *Experience and Nature* and *Art as Experience*. Despite Jackson's trained distrust of philosophy as unempirical, even fantastical, his yearning to attend to meaningful topics and issues led him to attend seriously to Dunkel's suggestion.

Shortly after, while on another sabbatical in Manchester, England, in 1968–1969, Jackson encountered a group of philosophers who were studying the writings of Ludwig Wittgenstein, in particular his *Tractatus* (1921/1961). Jackson found himself inexorably drawn to the difficult questions that form the core of Wittgenstein's work: What is language, and how does it affect thought and meaning? What is the relationship of the individual to the society? What are some alternative conceptions of intelligence that do not privilege logic or formal rationality? And what can we learn from those experiences that do not lend themselves to easy categorization or even description? These questions, along with his continued reading in Dewey, would come to play a central role in Jackson's subsequent move away from psychology and toward philosophy.

When Jackson returned to Chicago, he found himself faced with an unexpected challenge that took him temporarily away from his newfound interest in philosophy. The Laboratory School—founded by Dewey 80 years earlier—faced an administrative crisis, and provost John Wilson wanted Jackson to step into the role of director. Due more to his loyalty to the university than any great affinity for administration (but with the hope that the experience might provide him greater insights into the practical side of progressive education), Jackson agreed to commit 5 years to the job.

One of the items that Jackson often relates concerning this administrative experience was his discovery that the founder of the school was conspicuous mainly for being absent from the discussions and methods of the teachers. In response to this absence, Jackson instituted a series of faculty seminars in which the teachers were expected to read Dewey and think about the implications of his words for their teaching. Through this activity, Jackson soon learned that Dewey's writings had perhaps a greater potential for fostering teacher reflection than he had initially supposed.

In 1975, Jackson ended his brief tenure as Lab School director, accepting the chairmanship of the Department of Education and serving as the final dean of the soon-to-be-closed Graduate School of Education. By that time, Dunkel and his colleague Joseph Schwab had retired, so, owing to the recent shift in his intellectual horizons, Jackson assumed responsibility for teaching philosophy of education courses and for the supervision of graduate students in the Philosophy of Curriculum program in the Department of Education.

In the tradition of Dunkel and Schwab, Jackson chose to include Dewey's *School and Society*, *Child and the Curriculum*, and *Democracy and Education* in his introductory philosophy of education course. And by 1980, he was every other year or so teaching an advanced seminar on one or more of Dewey's later works. Jackson, understandably, had developed a particular interest in Dewey's *Human Nature and Conduct*, *Experience and Nature*, and *Art as Experience*, coming to believe that there was a coherent (if understated) worldview in those books with a power beyond that found in Dewey's more explicitly educational works. He would also find his own writing coming to embody many Deweyan elements and ideas.

JACKSON AS A DEWEYAN WRITER

Jackson is very much a performative writer. This is not to say that he attempts to put on a performance of some kind, like an entertainer playing before an audience and providing a reprieve from the trials and tedium of everyday life. It means, rather, that Jackson's writing typically communicates his thoughts and ideas through the activity of showing or pointing rather than direct saying. Indeed, it is frequently the case that what he wants to show or point out to us, though emphatically part of our everyday lives, cannot be directly said, at least not without substantially altering or diminishing its meaning. This is because Jackson's subject matter is often intellectually slippery or intractable, resisting concrete definition and description. To accommodate for this, Jackson works to orchestrate reading encounters (some might say conversations) in which we are called to participate with him in an experience, to share in it in some immediately meaningful and intellectually enlightening way. In responding to this call, moreover, we readily become participants in Jackson's ongoing investigations, even if we meet up with him midway through some seemingly ordinary, yet also inevitably extraordinary, line of inquiry. In this way we are able to share in his many insights, discoveries, and achievements, no less than his perplexities, confusions, and, occasionally, disappointments. Regardless of the direct outcome, we are commonly left with more than a few questions unanswered or settled only partially and provisionally. We also inevitably come away with a better understanding of the subject matter explored.

Dewey would surely appreciate Jackson's overarching purpose and methodology here. He, too, is deeply committed to the life-altering and life-affirming possibilities of shared experience. Such experience is for Dewey one of the great miracles of human existence. And as Jackson takes pains to point out, Dewey also defies conventional thinking in maintaining that language is much more than a means of conveying preformed observations and ideas. Instead, Dewey sees it as a transformative medium. That is to say, language, for Dewey, actively creates meaning and value in the process of creating participation in some shared life activity (Jackson, 1998b). This means that it is not primarily the quality of observations and ideas that determine the quality of a piece of writing; it is the quality of participatory experience fostered through these observations and ideas with readers. That said, Dewey nonetheless remains very conscious of the limits of language. He fully recognizes that experience in its qualitative immediacy—the stirring vibrancy of *that* night at the symphony or the strained look of frustration on *this* student's face—is ultimately ineffable, that it extends and resonates beyond the descriptive capacity of language (Jackson, 1998b). This in no way diminishes its potential meaning and significance, however, or the need in some way to acknowledge its existence. Quite the opposite, in fact, Jackson wants us to understand (1992b).

A principal feature of Dewey's philosophy is the notion that the directly "had" or felt meanings carried through this immediate, qualitative dimension of things make up the primary field and horizons of everyday experience. They, not the artifacts of some mode of knowing, constitute the basic existential conditions of human life and activity. In short, immediate sense-qualities are what we live in and for. "The world in which we immediately live, that in which we strive, succeed, and are defeated," writes Dewey, "is preeminently a qualitative world" (LW.10.297). All the same, Jackson powerfully demonstrates in *Life in Classrooms* (1968), *The Moral Life of Schools* (Jackson, Boostrom, & Hansen, 1993), *Untaught Lessons* (1992b), *John Dewey and the Lessons of Art* (1998b) and elsewhere that the things that are the most commonplace or ordinary are, in their very ordinariness, frequently the hardest for us to see or, more precisely, to perceive. As Wittgenstein once put it, "One is unable to notice something—because it is always before one's eyes" (Wittgenstein, 1953). And because things in their immediacy cannot be analyzed, measured, and quantified without being existentially compromised, because they cannot be intellectualized and known according to the tenets of scientific rationality, they are often treated as somewhat less than genuinely real. They become, in a word, merely subjective, and we become skeptics about their existence (Jackson, 1992b).

Dewey offers a corrective of sorts here, one that, as a plea for engagement in "the full range and total complexity of human affairs," Jackson (2002b) actively embraces in his work (p. 19). Refusing "the primacy and ultimacy of purely logical thought and its findings," Dewey claims that, "to settle any discussion, to still any doubt, to answer any question, we must [finally] go to something pointed to, denoted, and find our answer in that thing" (LW.1.372). This means that the directly "had" or felt dimension of experience must always and inevitably be both the beginning and end of inquiry. Moreover, it suggests that optimal human intelligence requires elements that might be called, depending on one's perspective, subrational or suprarational. And perhaps most notable of all, Dewey urges us to accept whatever is found through this pointing or showing "in good faith and without discount" (LW.1.372).

As Jackson (2002b) is quick to point out, this posture of "good faith" is not meant to signal the attainment of a fixed and final truth (p. 18). Such would certainly be anathema to Dewey and to any thoroughgoing empiricism. However it does mean that there are grounds for acting on the thing pointed to or shown, that some object or event really exists, even if our actions or inquiries subsequently lead us to amend our understanding of its meaning and value. Uncertainty, then, should not be taken—indeed, in the end, cannot be taken—

as an automatic prescription for inaction (Jackson, 2002b; pp. 18–20; see also Jackson, 1992b, pp. 1–19). To do so leads inevitably to a skeptical withdrawal from the everyday world of lived experience. It makes it impossible to respond genuinely and wholeheartedly to the full range and total complexity of human affairs.

So how can one use language to illuminate the meaning and significance of the qualitative dimension of things? There are two principal methods for doing so, as Dewey sees it. For intellectual purposes, he says, one can accomplish this by "giv[ing] directions as to how to come upon these qualities in experience" (LW.10.219). He also recommends that these directions be as simple and straightforward as possible. The more one tries to dictate and control the particulars of another's encounter with some experienced quality, the more likely these directions will "confuse instead of guiding" (LW.10.219–220). On the other hand, Dewey maintains that "words serve their poetic purpose in the degree in which they summon and evoke into active operation the vital responses that are present whenever we experience qualities" (LW.10.220). While the former method attends to experienced qualities indirectly, through the signifying capacity of language, the latter method evokes them directly, or, as we often say, "in the moment."

Both of these methods can readily be found in Jackson's writings. As avenues of shared experience, they greatly enhance his efforts to illuminate the meaning of objects or events in their immediacy and to draw our attention to their commonly overlooked or discounted, yet nonetheless important and consequential, features.

Much of the time, Jackson proceeds by examining the circumstances and significance of these objects or events within some shared form of life, such as teaching, research, the moral life, or the arts. To assist in this process, he routinely calls us to reflect on what initially seem to be rather simple, even mundane-sounding, questions—and sometimes a whole series of them. With these unassuming questions, however, Jackson deftly points us to aspects of things that we have likely never considered or paid serious attention to before. Instead of suggesting predetermined answers, giving us specific things to look for and neatly categorize or explain away, these questions invite continued reflection. They ask us, in effect, "What might it mean if we look at it this way?" or "What if this is really the case rather than that?"

On other occasions, Jackson's writing places us within the events of an unfolding narrative or "story" of some kind. Being thus situated, we are able to experience some range of designated qualities in a firsthand and immediately meaningful way. In other words, we are able to experience them through our own "vital responses" to the events undergone. In this manner also, Jackson is able, as Dewey says, "to give significance to descriptive and analytic terms otherwise meaningless" (LW.1.232). We understand, for instance, what it means to talk about the "unifying quality of emotion in experience" or how it serves to "filter our perceptions" when we are put in a position to experience directly and attend to these things ourselves (Jackson, 1998b, pp. 10–12).[1]

With either method, the meaning experienced by readers is robustly two-dimensional. It possesses considerable semantic breadth as well as depth. This is because Jackson's manner of writing effectively embodies what Dewey calls the "field structure" of consciousness (LW.1.231). That is to say, it purposively utilizes both a foreground of focal or discursive meanings and a more qualitative background of directly intuited or nondiscursive meanings. The latter intuited meanings serve to situate, augment, and embellish the focal or discursive meanings. In short, they suffuse Jackson's writing with a subtly nuanced and carefully crafted, yet also unmistakably organic, quality. They compel us to slow down as readers and to prepare ourselves for all manner of pregnant pauses and intermediary reflections. These intuited meanings are also enhanced by Jackson's deliberate avoidance of technical jargon and by his sensitivity and responsiveness to the myriad "overtones and resonances" of everyday words (LW.10.245). Nor do we sense any compulsion on his part to be discursively replete, to attempt to force all of the pertinent meanings into the semantic foreground. For Jackson writes in such a way that these unsaid, intuited meanings often become as important and consequential for our understanding, and indeed as present in our experience, as the literal or manifest content of his words. At such times the semantic foreground and background blend seamlessly together. What is more, this occurs without any significant loss or corruption of meaning. In fact the reverse is very much the case.

As Dewey tells it, this is precisely how the arts work. The arts, he says, accentuate, clarify, and intensify the meanings of objects and events in their immediacy. They crack the shell of mundaneness that we tend to build around everyday things, allowing us to "share vividly and deeply in meanings to which we had become dumb" (LW.10.248). The skeptic desires complete certainty in his commerce with his surroundings; his is a reality that ultimately turns on fixed meanings and values. Thus he is often led to think that the world—including the processes of teaching and learning—can only be disclosed through the most rigorous (read positivistic) science, through what the poet William Blake called "The Atoms of Democritus / And Newton's Particles of light" (quoted in Jackson, 1990b, p. xi; see also Jackson, 1992b, pp. 21–23). The Deweyan alternative, and that which is epitomized in much of Jackson's work, "accepts life and experience in all its uncertainty, mystery, doubt, and half-knowledge and turns that experience upon itself to deepen and intensify its own qualities—to imagination and art" (LW.10.41). In other words, it takes the limits and liabilities of the human condition and turns them into poetic affirmations. The aesthetic and moral meanings that result are, for Dewey and

Jackson, no less revelatory of the lived world than the august laws of physics and mathematics. They, too, have a great deal to teach us.

There are clearly a great many Deweyan elements and ideas in evidence in Jackson's writings. We have also seen that they run deeper than his stated subject matter and extend well beyond his nominally Deweyan books and essays. It can seem rather curious, then, that Jackson and Dewey are at the same time stylistically very different writers and, in certain affiliated ways, different thinkers as well. There are likely a variety of reasons for this, both personal and professional, but only one need concern us here. This is that Dewey and Jackson have taken on somewhat different (though plainly compatible) emphases as writers and thinkers. In his major philosophic works, Dewey tends to operate at a very high level of abstraction, surveying and mapping the general terrain of selected portions of the lived world. His purpose is to scout out suitable paths from one point to another and to identify the major landmarks along the way, all the while keeping an eye on their embodiment in ordinary affairs (see Jackson, 1998b, pp. 33–34, 161). The resulting maps, Dewey offers, "may be of assistance to the direct experience of others, as a survey of a country is of help to the one who travels through it" (LW.10.313). Jackson is doing something similar in his work, no doubt; however, his inquiries tend to commence from and revolve around situational contexts that are more local and concrete in nature. In his writings on Dewey, accordingly, Jackson journeys through and explores select portions of these maps with his readers. Along the way, he looks to fill in some of the relevant details and particulars as they emerge within specific experiential or situational contexts (especially with respect to teaching and research) and as they are embodied in ordinary affairs. He is also not averse to augmenting or emending Dewey's maps where he finds it propitious to do so. With that in mind, the remainder of this essay will briefly recount some of the highlights of Jackson's journeys along two pivotal segments of Dewey's maps—those charting the intersecting terrain of Dewey's metaphysics and his aesthetics.

METAPHYSICS AND THE FORMS OF EXPERIENCE

Almost from the beginning, Jackson's careful reading in Dewey deepened his interest in the possibility of maintaining a naturalistic, or empirical, method of inquiry while avoiding the reductionism of so much educational research. He wanted to find ways to study human nature, teaching, learning, and reality itself in general without becoming so abstract as to lose the ability to bring such generalizations back to particular problems of practice. Dewey, as we have seen, had pursued the same goal, resulting eventually in *Experience and Nature*, a book that continues to generate considerable controversy for violating the neopragmatic principle that all truth claims are local and contingent. Jackson was particularly troubled by Richard Rorty's dismissal, in 1977, of Dewey's empirical metaphysics as an outright "mistake." Rorty's criticisms struck him as too facile and as ignoring the fact that Dewey devoted many years to developing and refining his metaphysical methods and conclusions. Jackson had become convinced that Dewey was acting more than willfully in being so consistently drawn to such abstract topics as "the nature of existences of all kinds regardless." He was thus ready for the more favorable treatment of Dewey's metaphysics offered in Jim Garrison's 1985 article, "Dewey and the Empirical Unity of Opposites," Ralph Sleeper's *The Necessity of Pragmatism* (1986), and Raymond Boisvert's *Dewey's Metaphysics* (1988).

By the late 1980s, Jackson had come to believe that serious close study of *Experience and Nature* could result in new understandings about the nature of existence and, in particular, about the importance of qualitative immediacy in human experience. These interests even led him to steer several graduate students in the direction of Dewey's metaphysical works and ideas. In the meantime, Jackson was himself busy studying *Experience and Nature*, especially the variations in Dewey's successive attempts to introduce the difficult volume. This led to his 1999 John Dewey Society lecture, which was subsequently to become the 2002 publication, *John Dewey and the Philosopher's Task*.

John Dewey and the Philosopher's Task (2002b) epitomizes the singular performative quality of Jackson's work. In this book, Jackson proposes to "share my own sense of puzzlement as it emerged for me during my reading of" *Experience and Nature* (Jackson 2002b, p. 3). In the course of articulating and reflecting on his own puzzlement with Dewey's method, he invites the reader to travel with him on a philosophical journey of self-discovery, while along the way revealing a good deal of what Dewey himself had discovered during his repeated attempts to introduce his metaphysical study. Jackson also demonstrates an approach to textual study that takes curiosity—or inquisitiveness—as the ultimate method, driven by the hope that continual questioning and hypothesizing will bear both intrinsic and extrinsic rewards.

Throughout this period, Jackson's interest in Dewey's metaphysics never centered on the precise conclusions that Dewey draws about the nature of nature or, as he commonly calls it, the generic traits of existences. (Jackson was happy to allow others, including his own students, to worry about that.) Rather, he was most intrigued by the question of why someone so explicitly devoted to empirical naturalism would even care to engage in such a high level of abstraction and generality. In other words, how is it possible for Dewey to combine a metaphysical orientation with a genuinely empirical method? And what is the payoff of serious empirical study at the highest level of generality? (See Jackson, 2002b, p. 7.) In asking these questions, Jackson is more concerned with the work being done by the philosopher-as-metaphysician than he is with the specific results of such work. His published writing on Dewey's metaphysics is therefore devoted to a kind of intellectual biography, not for the sake of chronology or genealogy, but instead to uncover and explore deeper discomforts and motivations, ultimately as a means for better understanding his own thinking.

By 2002, Jackson had arrived at what he considered to be a satisfactory understanding of what Dewey was seeking: a naturalistic sense of the potential meanings and purposes of human life. To reach this point, he focused on what Dewey had called the "forms of experience"—what Jackson preferred to describe as practices and behaviors that transcend the particular details of specific contexts to become almost archetypes of human striving to understand and to experience their full humanity. These forms are prephilosophical; that is to say, human experience comes to us prepackaged in such groupings. The forms or groupings are crucial in that they provide the philosophical inquirer with much-needed leverage in deciding how to proceed in coming to understand the nature of experience in general.

In *John Dewey and the Philosopher's Task* and more recent writings, Jackson has identified several interlocking processes that have this archetypal quality: science, art, democracy, morality, politics, education, and religion. These processes constitute means for individuals to grow—to transcend their present selves so as to more fully realize their potential selves. The processes, seemingly by their very natures and despite often being co-opted for narrow instrumental ends, inexorably generate intelligence, community, and the possibility of freedom. They are, then, the preeminent human-made tools of positive personal and social transformation.

In seeking to identify a suitable end-point to Dewey's struggle to contextualize his metaphysical work, Jackson also embodies Dewey's own metaphor for the philosopher's task—that of the mapmaker. Using interpolation and triangulation (based on his broad and detailed understanding of Dewey's work as a whole, an understanding that likely exceeds Dewey's own sense of the "drift and hang" of his philosophy toward the end of his life), Jackson is able to improve upon Dewey's own metaphysical map. In a word, he shows us that the map is not simply descriptive with regard to the forms of experience but "also theoretical in outlook and therefore imaginatively productive" (2002b, p. 14). "Its 'issue,' as Dewey said at the start, is no less than a theory of nature, the world, the universe." Further, Jackson's revised version of the map meets Dewey's own criteria of being "critical, evaluative, and judgmental," thus potentially fulfilling philosophy's "function as a humane undertaking"—a form of applied intelligence (2002b, pp. 14–15).

The processes or practices selected by Jackson are, of course, the processes that Dewey himself came to see as worthy of intensive study—not so much for what they are, again, but rather for the potentialities they offer for the improvement of personal and institutional habits. This explains, to some degree, the fact that Dewey's writings strayed noticeably away from explicit attention to education per se in his later period. It wasn't so much that Dewey had been a failure at educational reform as that Dewey began to understand that education really is coterminous with life itself. He saw, too, that to understand or improve education, you need to understand the nature of habits, intelligence, experience, and reality, as well as the major modes in which humans strive to make sense of it all.

Jackson's career has followed a very similar path, in search not only of what makes for good teaching and learning but also of what human nature is and what the nature of reality is that makes teaching and learning possible. Thus, for Jackson as well as for Dewey, metaphysical excursions have been part of an intelligent and coherent plan for social melioration. Having provided the field of education with a "ground-map of the province of criticism," Dewey and Jackson have dramatically increased the possibilities of social melioration, without necessarily telling us exactly what to do as we try "to make life better for [ourselves] and for others through an artful blend of thought, feeling, and action" (Jackson, 2002b, p. 101).[2]

JACKSON, DEWEY, AND THE LESSONS OF ART

Though his interest in the arts comprises a long and eventful history, Jackson's journey into Dewey's aesthetics began formally and in earnest with an article entitled "If We Took Dewey's Aesthetics Seriously, How Would Art Be Taught?" (1995).[3] Jackson explains that his motivation for writing this particular piece, which served as a scouting mission of sorts for the project that later culminated in *John Dewey and the Lessons of Art* (1998b), stemmed from the disturbing fact that art educators have by and large ignored Dewey's aesthetics. What is more, Jackson (1995) tells us, "not only do art educators have much to gain from reading [Dewey's] *Art as Experience* and taking its lessons to heart, we all do" (p. 25). Thus another of Jackson's purposes is to introduce and make Dewey's aesthetics available to a wider audience, one that extends beyond departments of philosophy and the cloistered halls of the academy. Indeed, he rightly points out that Dewey's standing and influence as a philosopher, as well as a public intellectual, was actually on the downturn by the time *Art as Experience*, his only extended work on the arts, was published in 1934. (Dewey was 75 at the time.) Nor, sadly, did the book receive a particularly warm reception among academics of the day (Jackson, 1998b, pp. xi–xii).

More recently, as we saw above, Jackson (2002b) has been exploring the hypothesis that Dewey's philosophical allegiance over the years moved gradually away from the sciences and toward the humanities (p. 96). His emerging sense of this subtle shift, along with his awareness of the iconoclastic tendencies of more recent, so called post-historical movements in the arts, might also explain Jackson's desire with *John Dewey and the Lessons of Art* to give Dewey's aesthetics a deep and sustained look, perhaps more so than might otherwise have been called for. Still another catalyst, as Jackson tells it, is the curious (though not entirely inexplicable) fact that Dewey says almost nothing in *Art as Experience* about the educational implications of his aesthetics. (He suggests that Dewey had neither the time nor means at that point in his life to flesh out these implications to his satisfaction [1998b].) And while Jackson himself demurs at the possibility of an "applied" version of *Art as Experience*, he does speak at length about the broader implications of Dewey's aesthetics "for the general reader and especially for educators"—among them, as we shall soon see, Dewey himself (1998b).

One of the defining characteristics of Dewey's aesthetics concerns the way the arts function as a medium of expression. For it is through the qualitative immediacy of expressive meanings that objects and events of various kinds become, in his words, "the matter of a clarified, coherent, and intensified or 'impassioned' experience" (LW.10.295). Jackson's interest in these expressive meanings clearly encompasses the arts, especially as they are paradigmatic of this aesthetic experience. Like Dewey, then, he attends first and foremost to what he calls, for the sake of expedience, "art-centered experience" (1998b). Yet also congruent with Dewey's map of the terrain, Jackson's interest extends liberally to contexts of everyday life in their aesthetic and moral dimensions, including, of course, schools and classrooms. Thus Jackson makes much of the fact that expressive meanings become embedded in objects and events not only through the singular skills and efforts of artists but also through the purposive cycle of doing (acting) and undergoing (being acted upon) that constitutes our daily interactions with the people and things that make up our everyday environments. This means that the expressive qualities of things, the qualities that give them intrinsic meaning and value, are, in Jackson's words, "infinitely expandable" and that they owe their existence in large part to "the world we share with others" (1995, p. 32). One of the things that the arts might teach us, accordingly, is how better to cultivate, attend to, and appreciate such qualities.

One important group of writers that held a deep appreciation for the educative potency of the expressive meanings that come to inhere in everyday objects and events was the English Romantic poets, especially Wordsworth, Coleridge, and Keats. (Emerson could easily be included here as well.) They are also, for this and related reasons, favorites of Dewey's and Jackson's. As teachers of a kind, the Romantics dedicated themselves to awakening us to those often-elusive meanings of things that lie, as it were, beneath or beyond

the surface of our habitual or customary way of looking at things—the domain of the extraordinary in the ordinary. Philosopher Stanley Cavell's (1986)
gloss on Wordsworth's formulation vis-à-vis the ordinary is keenly illustra-
tive here: "The common world, the world common to us, is as it stands of
no interest to us, that it is no longer ours, that we are as if bored quite to
death, and that poetry has nominated itself to bring us back from this 'torpor'" (p. 186).

Jackson believes that Dewey articulates something analogous in *Art as
Experience*. Simply put, he sees Dewey as a willing inheritor of the poet's
cause, a dedicated ally in the Romantic's project to "rescue" the "sense of the
familiar . . . from the oblivion" of the mind's "savage torpor" (LW.10.145). The
way the common world—as, literally, our commonwealth—stands to us is
largely up to how we stand to it, Dewey, Jackson, and the Romantics want us
to understand. It is a function of our ability to experience our surroundings
in all of their fecundity, to perceive them not through the attenuated lens of
a coldly detached and dispassionate objectivity (what Emerson calls "paltry
empiricism"), but rather with the sensitivity and attunement of an expansive,
feeling intellect. Learning to perceive the world in this way is, for Dewey and
Jackson, a critical component of aesthetic education in the broadest sense.
Nor is it only of relevance for students and teachers. As we observed earlier,
Jackson believes that all of us who care about how schools and teachers are
really affecting our students might profitably work to develop a heightened
sensitivity to the subtleties and nuances of school and classroom life, to those
things that normally pass us by unnoticed. For only in doing so can we truly
recognize and appreciate those intangible outcomes of schooling that, as
Jackson's work repeatedly demonstrates, shape us in sometimes profound
ways (for better or for worse) as human beings yet that have inevitably "eluded
our nation's test-makers and pollsters" (Jackson, 1992b, p. 90).

Jackson then adds a point of emphasis here that bears repeating. He
observes that the reigning philosophy of consciousness leads us to think of
experience of all types, cognitive and noncognitive, as essentially psychological phenomena. Experience, in this view, is said to occur exclusively within
us, or, more specifically, in our minds or heads. Hence it is typically seen as
a private (subjective) affair, one constituted of discrete units of sense data
or some other psychological atoms, while the (objective) world is presumed
to exist "out there" somewhere. For Dewey and Jackson, however, experience emerges out of our embodied, purposive, and ongoing interactions with
the people and things around us (Jackson, 1995, p. 26). In this more fully
contextualized view of experience, the world is an environment that we inhabit in and through our habits—call it our habitat—not a picture of some
kind that we behold across a gaping ontological divide. "It is not experience
which is experienced," Dewey writes, "but nature—stones, plants, animals,

diseases, health, temperature, electricity, and so on. Things interacting in certain ways *are* experience; they are what is experienced" (quoted in Jackson, 1998b, p. 2). This means that art resides neither in the "eye of the beholder" nor in some outer material essence, but rather, as Jackson (2002a) reports in his analysis of Dewey's brief 1906 definition of art, in the achieved unity of subject and object, self and world (p. 176). Here is Dewey's definition in full: "To feel the meaning of what one is doing, and to rejoice in that meaning; to unite in one concurrent fact the unfolding of the inner life and the ordered development of material conditions—that is art" (quoted in Jackson, 2002a, p. 167). Jackson believes that there is more than ample room here to accommodate the fine and performing arts as well as the art of (and in) teaching and learning. Indeed, the definition is virtually homologous with what Dewey honorifically dubs, in *Experience and Education*, an "educative experience" (LW.13.26–27). By presenting art as "central to a model of human flourishing," Jackson (2002a) says, it constitutes a "step in the direction of demystifying art with a capital A, while at the same time democratizing it" (p. 176).

We have seen that Jackson (1998b) very much shares Dewey's belief that perception has a certain redemptive potency in that it can afford us a new and revitalized perspective on the things of everyday life, perhaps leading us to attend to these things in a different, more appreciative and solicitous, even more moral way (pp. 156–158). What is more, Jackson argues that, on rare occasions, art-centered experiences can take on a pronounced spiritual quality. By this he means that they can radically and irrevocably transform our way of being in the world, even if, with many contemporary artworks, they do not provide the degree of experienced unity and closure that Dewey theorizes (1998b, p. 112). The act of perception, then, is fundamentally educative in nature; and it can serve equally well instrumental and aesthetic or moral ends. Yet Jackson also reminds us that any genuine act of perception takes work and that given the patience and persistence, the fairness and sense of caring it requires, it is itself an inherently moral act (Jackson et al., 1993, p. 94). Recognizing things, naming and categorizing them according to a fixed perspective and stock interpretation of some kind, is a largely automatic and perfunctory activity. But to perceive something in the Deweyan sense, to partake of its meaning and value as it exists in the concrete here-and-now, is considerably more demanding. It is something, notes Jackson (1998b), that we must learn, and regularly relearn, how to do through continued practice, something requiring that we develop and refine our habits of perception over time (p. 57).

It is not surprising, then, that Jackson's evolving explanations and exemplifications of the work of perception help to flesh out Dewey's assertion that habits are at bottom "arts" of a kind. Habits can rightly be conceived as arts, according to Dewey, in that they are human creations that shape and order the environment as we encounter it in lived experience. When intelligently developed and flexibly responsive, these habits-as-arts (including those that make up our perceptual aptitudes) enhance our ability to interact meaningfully and resourcefully with this environment. In a word, they increase our opportunities for finding and creating meaning in the world (MW.14.15–16, 31). Add to this Dewey's contention that habits largely constitute the self, and we can begin to understand why Jackson regularly portrays the activities of teaching and research using language and concepts common within the arts (including literature and poetry). Here, for example, is the way Jackson (1986) describes the perceptual activity of an "expert" teacher (and which might, with minor modifications, also describe an "expert" Jacksonian researcher):

> Expert teachers "see more" than do nonexperts. They are alive to the latent pedagogical possibilities in the events they witness. Within a classroom setting, they anticipate what is going to happen. They can spot an inattentive student a mile off. They can detect signs of incipient difficulty. Their senses are fully tuned to what is going on around them. They are not easily rattled. As younger students sometimes swear is true, they behave as though they had eyes in the back of their heads. (p. 87)

This description contrasts sharply with Dewey's brief sketch of the opposite sort of teacher, one whose behaviors are more or less automated and mechanical. Of this person he writes, "If the action of a teacher is so fluent as to exclude emotional and imaginative perception of what he is doing, he may be safely set down as a wooden and perfunctory pedagogue" (LW.10.267).

On that note, as Jackson asks, what can we say about Dewey himself as a classroom teacher? Did he apply the lessons of art (as he would come to know them) to his own teaching and successfully engage his students in the types of exemplary experiences that he associates with the arts? Were the students' experiences infused with a fertile blend of immediately enjoyed and instrumental meanings, for example, and did the students play an active role in shaping and guiding these experiences? In short, what was the culture of experience like in Dewey's classroom?

Jackson's mostly negative judgment must surely come as a surprise and disappointment to many readers, especially given Dewey's repeated admonishments concerning the integration of theory and practice. For it seems that Dewey was not very mindful of his students as they sat before him, of their interests and ideas and their capacity to follow his allegedly serpentine lectures. Indeed, he often appeared to them essentially lost in thought. If the reports of some of his former students are to be believed, he even failed to make eye contact on a regular basis or to make sufficient room for students' questions and comments (Jackson, 1998b, pp. 182–186).

As harsh as this brief depiction sounds—and Jackson freely concedes as much—it does not exactly make Dewey a "wooden and perfunctory pedagogue." For these same reports also portray him as someone who was clearly emotionally and imaginatively engaged in his work. Indeed, what Dewey was doing in his "lectures," the students (at least some of them) eventually realized, was demonstrating aloud the difficult work of open and honest inquiry—what Emerson calls "Man Thinking"—albeit unannounced and without adequate explanation. Moreover, he was doing so using genuinely felt problems with which he was actually struggling at the time (Jackson, 1998b, pp. 184-190). Jackson likens Dewey's "thinking aloud" pedagogy to a writer or artist at work. He notes, for instance, that it evidences the same mental absorption, intense concentration, and loss of self-consciousness (1998b, p. 191). The chief problem with this behavior, from an educational standpoint, is that Dewey failed to include the students as part of the material and resources with which he was working. Dewey recognized the students, as Jackson puts it, but he did not fully perceive them. The students' presence in the classroom as living creatures ultimately made little difference to Dewey's actions. He remained essentially "*unattached* to them, emotionally distant" (Jackson, 1998b, p. 193; emphasis in original).

Why was Dewey not more attentive and responsive as a teacher? Was he not aware of his pedagogical shortcomings? And why did he fail for the most part to apply the lessons of art to his own teaching? Jackson admits that he does not rightly know. Yet he remains confident that we might profitably learn from Dewey's mistakes and attempt to pick up where he left off. There is much promising work yet to be done, Jackson believes, as we each navigate our way across Dewey's critical-creative maps of human possibility.

CONCLUSION: FINDING/MAKING OUR WAY IN THE WORLD

In his Preface to *Elements of the Philosophy of Right*, G. W. F. Hegel (1821/1991) writes that "the owl of Minerva begins its flight only with the onset of dusk" (p. 23). Minerva, you will recall, was the ancient Roman goddess of wisdom, also identified with the Greek goddess Athena. Hegel's famous words suggest that the philosophical understanding or wisdom of a culture is fully realized only after that culture has entered its twilight years. Jackson has said that these words also speak in a way to the philosophical journey that he has taken over the years, and he tells us that the same could be said of Dewey's journey. Jackson reports that, much like Dewey, he has only really come to understand the "'drift and hang of the various positions [he has] taken'" with the benefit of hindsight and the wisdom and perspective it affords (quoted in Jackson, 2002b, p. 56). As we have seen, a regular theme of this journey for both travelers has been the ongoing struggle to understand the relative places and purposes of philosophy, science, and the arts in human affairs. However, for much of the time, we are told, this struggle appeared only as so many smaller and more immediate questions and problems. Its larger form and contours were for many years only dimly and tenuously perceived. Dewey's poetic imagery and motifs for the work of philosophy, his recurring metaphors of a ship at sea or the handheld candle of the lonely traveler, reflect this admixture of illumination and darkness. As Jackson (1982) observes:

> Both the ship and the light are weak. Both are buffeted by the elements. Neither the person aboard the ship nor the person holding the candle is at all certain as to where he is headed. The only decision for him to make is whether to turn this way or that for the next step or two, if on land, or how to avoid the obstacle ahead, if afloat. (p. 75)

This, indeed, would seem to be the condition of all of us who wish to live reflectively without the pretensions and apparatus of certainty—without, for example, the kind of psychological atomism that Dewey helped Jackson to exchange for a more holistic and inclusive idiom. It is the kind of journey that attends the search for continual enlightenment by living fully in the moment, propelled by a blend of intellectual courage and humility and guided by an end-in-view that must be repeatedly established and reestablished (Jackson, 2002b, p. 76). The risks are doubtless considerable, Jackson reports, but so are the potential rewards. For only in becoming more attuned to the full range and total complexity of human affairs in this way can we become sufficiently attuned to the extraordinary in the ordinary.

Finding Phil

Elliot W. Eisner

W HAT YOU are about to read is a personal story. I can tell it no other way. I have known Phil Jackson since 1956; if my watch is right, that's half a century. He served on my dissertation committee and provided a special kind of mentorship from the beginning. Despite the sense of warmth that I feel toward Phil—indeed, the sense of intimacy that we share—my comments will be no encomium. I want to share with you experiences that I believe say a lot about the person we are honoring in this Festschrift.

On this topic at least, I can do it no other way. There are dozens of scholars who could give you an analysis of his theoretical and empirical work. What such scholars cannot provide that I can are some of the personal events that populate our almost half-century journey.

Phil came to the University of Chicago only a couple of years before I did, and soon after we both arrived he was blessed—or you might say cursed—by fame. The fame that I speak of is the notoriety he received for his study of the relationship between creativity and intelligence. It was a study that was done with Jack Getzels, a Chicago colleague and another person who influenced my academic life. Jackson's interest in the measurement of intelligence and creativity and the study of their relationship was not surprising. He had studied, after all, with Irving Lorge, a psychometrician at Teachers College, Columbia University, and brought with him to the University of Chicago the tools and, to a large degree, although not entirely, the perspective that those tools adumbrated. Studying the world empirically meant for most scholars at that time studying it quantitatively. What you can't measure, you can't really know, or so it seemed to many.

Creativity and intelligence got a lot of play. It was an important topic for empirical study ever since J. P. Guilford's *The Structure of Intellect* was published in 1950. The tasks that were dreamed up to measure creative thinking were sexy, attractive, and often humorous. It seemed like a real breakthrough was being made to disaggregate intelligent behaviors from creative ones. It is a study that I think Phil would not like to be known for today. But when one is in one's thirties, or almost so, and your research gets reported in *Time* magazine, the trip is very heady indeed. A more sober Jackson would express reservations that apparently eluded both Getzels and Jackson in the 1950s.

There are two occasions during that early period in my career and indeed in his that I want to comment on. In 1960 I was an instructor in the School of Art at Ohio State University. Phil was invited to Columbus to give a talk there. He talked, not unexpectedly, about his work on creativity and intelligence. During the question-and-answer period, someone in the audience asked him, "What's your reason for doing this research?" His response, which I will never forget, was, "To satisfy my curiosity—is there any other reason?" The idea that ideas and problems could be pursued for their own sake, a lesson that exemplifies an aesthetic or artistic attitude toward making anything, simply had not really occurred to me until Phil encapsulated the idea in that very short response to a student's question. Teachers teach in many ways, and very often the most important lessons they teach are ones that they do not know that they have taught.

Related to their creativity and intelligence work was an invitation that Getzels and Jackson had received to speak to the Association for Supervision and Curriculum Development (ASCD), a large professional association consisting of curriculum directors, school administrators, and elementary and secondary school teachers. For whatever reason, they decided to turn down the invitation. I don't know whether there was a conflict in dates or meeting times or what, but they suggested to the people at ASCD that they get in touch with me since at that time I was working on a dissertation having to do with the analysis and measurement of types of creativity. They did, and I, of course, could not bypass the opportunity to give a public address to a large audience. The public address was given in the Grand Ballroom of the Hilton Hotel in Chicago to approximately 2,000 people. I wrote a 45-page paper that I was going to deliver in 50 minutes. That alone should indicate how much I knew about public speaking! In addition, since I had collected the data, I felt obligated to report the magnitude of the correlation coefficients and the variance accounted for by the factors that I had identified. All of this technical mumbo-jumbo in the context of 45 pages was to be delivered to 2,000 elementary and secondary school teachers and curriculum developers. I learned a lot, and although I lost some of the audience in the process, most hung in there with me. Maybe they were tired. In any case, Phil and Jack Getzels had opened a door for me.

There are a couple of other lessons that Phil taught me, not the least of which was that learning to write is really an exercise in learning how to think. There was no one on my committee—which consisted of Phil, John Goodlad, Joseph Schwab, and Maurice Hartung, a specialist in mathematics education—who was as demanding and as rigorous as Phil, except perhaps Schwab. When the two of them got through with my prose, there was hardly anything left.

I remember bringing him what I thought was a pretty well completed dissertation proposal. It really got masticated. When it became obvious that a substantial revision would need to be made, I commented to Phil that "I'll bring back a completed revised version in 2 weeks." My cocky self at age 26 felt assured that I could do a completed acceptable proposal in a couple of weeks, especially since I had done what I thought was almost a complete draft. To make a long story short, it took me 3 months to do what I thought was going to take 2 weeks. And I must confess I was the better for it.

Phil had a way of providing feedback that was quite interesting, to put it mildly. I remember walking into his office to get feedback on my dissertation. He had recorded his comments on a tape recorder and, rather than giving me written comments, he played his dictation just to make sure that I got the full force of his annoyance with what I had written! Another lesson that was unforgettable. To provide such feedback today in full force by voice in a support group–minded culture like the kind we have at Stanford would seem like a form of child abuse.

But the most significant critique that Phil provided to me occurred in the context of his smelling something rotten in the state of Denmark—and in this case, Denmark was located in a part of my dissertation. Believe it or not, my dissertation was a factor-analytic study of four types of creativity displayed in two kinds of art objects that were made by elementary school children. Because my mathematical aptitudes were never strong, I had asked a fellow student (who is now a very prominent educational researcher) to handle the factor analysis for me and to give me a correlation matrix that would enable me to generate an intelligent psychological interpretation of the factors that I had identified. For whatever reason, and I do not know what that reason was, Phil thought there was something wrong with the matrix and therefore with the factors, so he sent my raw data to Benjamin Wright, a high-powered quantitative methodologist working in the Department of Education at Chicago. Wright confirmed Phil's suspicion, and although I had written three chapters interpreting the significance and meaning of the correlation coefficients and the factors that were "discovered," I needed to redo the entire effort.

What had happened was that my erstwhile peer who, as I mentioned, is now a very prominent researcher in education, had put the 1st variable in the 14th field in the matrix and the 14th variable in the 1st field, so that each of the 14 variables in my study was misidentified; since I was interpreting the coefficients and factors on the basis of what I thought they were about, all the conclusions were wrong. Phil's keen eye picked it up. No one on the committee besides him had a clue.

Phil's most important work, at least in the early period, as far as I am concerned is *Life in Classrooms* (1968). You have to understand that *Life in Classrooms* is a study about classrooms in the Laboratory School of the University of Chicago. You also need to know that the Laboratory School is physically adjacent to the Department of Education. One might think that professors of education concerned with the improvement of schooling would take advantage of the convenient opportunity to study educational practice located right next door. This was not the case. For most faculty members, the Laboratory School could have been located in Montana or Maine; it would have made no difference. What Phil and a few others at the time initiated was the direct observation of "life in classrooms." He was interested in trying to find out what goes on in those places that theoreticians write about and that behavioral psychologists try to measure.

What Phil succeeded in doing was to recognize what is subtle but significant in the conduct of classroom life, and he had the perceptivity and literary skills to describe those features in a prose that made them memorable. Who can forget "the daily grind"? Who can forget the importance of students learning how to delay gratification? Who can forget the aroma, or should I say odor, of a place that smells of stale milk and that leaves chalk dust on your sleeves? For me the ability to notice what does not scream out at you and to reveal through language its presence and meaning is close to what I call connoisseurship and criticism. Phil might not be happy with those terms, but at base that is what he was doing. And because he saw what people may have noticed but were not conscious of and because he could create the right metaphor or capture the right image, his work stuck. The recent republication of *Life in Classrooms* is simply an indication of what most people who know the literature pertaining to classroom life recognize as a classic.

It is interesting to me that the quantitative data that are used in *Life in Classrooms* do not have—at least as I see it—the impact of Jackson's prose. Talking about stale milk and chalk dust serves to capture classroom conditions on the one hand and on the other to stimulate consciousness of what one has "known"—but not really.

You will recall my mentioning that when Phil Jackson came out of the chute with his new doctoral degree from Teachers College, he was socialized in quantitative forms of research. Something happened, though, on the road to Damascus. The world shifted, at least the research world shifted, for Phil from wanting to measure and nail down to wanting to describe and interpret. As he once mentioned to me, he found his métier in research and it was not the correlation matrix, it was the essay. If you look at his work, particularly over the past few years, you will see that it is the essay that encapsulates what he wants to talk about. In finding the essay as the means for revealing his expressive impulses, he moved from a quantitative psychology to a humanistic or literary form of intellectual life. His work is a lot closer to what one might find in *The New York Review of Books* than it is to the contents of the *American Educational Research Journal*. What characterizes his work for me, certainly in the past 20 or so years, is the depth of his insight and the acuteness of his observations. He takes on tasks that may look simple but does what most good teachers do—he makes them complex. I sometimes tell my own doctoral students at Stanford that "I am here to complicate your life." What I am after is providing them with some bones that they can gnaw on for the rest of their life. That image, indeed that aspiration, I can't help but think was stimulated, not explicitly but implicitly, by Phil's mentorship.

I have given you some sense of what Phil has been to me as a mentor and as a teacher, but as important as these roles are, they are exceeded by what Phil has been to me as a friend. Phil struggles with the tension between being intellectually honest and rigorous and his recognition that friendship sometimes requires an emphasis on other, more forgiving human virtues— kindness, for example. I wouldn't describe Phil as kind; at least it's not the first descriptor that comes to mind. I would describe him as tough—but considerate. This toughness and consideration are displayed in a recurrent experience we have been having over the past decade or so. We talk to each other at least monthly. "How are you doing?" I ask, expecting his usual answer, "I'm hanging in there." But these pleasantries are simply the initiating conditions of intellectually challenging and genuinely interesting ideas, conundrums, problems, dilemmas, puzzlements, contradictions, and the like. In short, we talk a kind of educational philosophy about what we are struggling with and about what matters most to us. For example, we can very easily spend an hour on the phone discussing whether John Dewey thought some works of art were better than others. Although the answer might seem obvious to the layperson, let me assure you that it is not. And even though I have spent almost 40 years struggling with such ideas, like a great piece of music, they are very difficult to exhaust.

The turn to the essay as his expressive structure has also represented a turn to philosophical considerations. He reads Kant in German at night, sometimes for pleasure, sometimes because he can't sleep, and at other times because he is struggling with a problem that will not let go. As for the sleep problem, I have offered him some of my own papers and some term papers as a surefire remedy for insomnia. Apparently he doesn't need them. What I find in Phil are opportunities to be engaged intellectually, opportunities that are all too rare in my experience working in universities. There is, of course, the occasional conversation, often in or near the men's room or on the stairs going to or leaving it. But these abortive practices do not begin to characterize what Phil and I have as intellectual exchange. In some magical way, our pleasantries get transformed, and rather quickly, into unanswerable questions, which, of course, are in the end the only ones worth asking.

But our relationship as friends is not only intellectual, it is one pervaded by mutual respect and by love. We love each other. There, I said it. No need to be embarrassed. It's not a bad thing if you can get it.

This state of our relationship gets strengthened annually at AERA meetings, or at least when Phil attends them, which is more frequent now than it was at one time. How does that relationship get strengthened? On a bench. When we are at AERA meetings, we look for a bench. Some people would give their kingdom for a horse. We would give ours for a bench. We find a bench and sit and talk, and talk, and talk. It is a traveling seminar that meets annually and, I must tell you, membership in this club is filled. There we are, just two friends, talking intently about things that matter to us.

Sometimes, but not all that often, conversation turns to personal matters. How the family is in more than a trivial way. How we are. When you have passed three score and ten, health is always an issue. And so we meet, we sit, we talk, we argue. Sometimes we even give each other sufficient space to allow each of us to play our favorite cello for some period of time. Talking things out solo is one way to try to understand what one is talking about.

Phil's major love outside of his family is the world of John Dewey. I know of no one in the field of education who has such a detailed and intimate grasp of Dewey, his life, his family, his context, his strengths, his weaknesses, his love affairs, his intellectual work. Yes, Dewey had love affairs! In fact, I would say that Dewey is planted so firmly on Phil Jackson's back that at times Phil would like to get him off. I say fat chance of that.

So to sum up, it is for all of the foregoing reasons and ones that are ineffable that Phil holds an important, indeed a precious, role in my life, first as a student, then as a colleague, and now as a friend. He is a tough-minded scholar, a passionate person, and a caring human being. He loves ideas and loves talking with those he respects about mutual intellectual interests. He has given me more than I can repay, although I am sure he has no expectation of repayment of any kind. He is a person who has helped expand the focus of research in education, not by excluding conventional ways of doing research but by opening up a place for narrative. Phil Jackson has helped us notice what life in classrooms is like, and noticing is the beachhead that must be established for any conceptual work to have grounding. Phil Jackson has provided much of the grounding.

As important as these contributions might be to the field, it is the personal connections that mean the most to me. I am looking forward to their continuation. Phil, I scouted around the neighborhood and have already located a bench for the two of us. There are a couple of points you made in your last paper that I want to take issue with.

Notes

CHAPTER 2

1. References to Dewey's scholarship in the volume are from the critical (print) edition, *The Collected Works of John Dewey, 1882-1953*, edited by Jo Ann Boydston and published by Southern Illinois University Press, Carbondale (1969-1991). The works have appeared in three series, *The Early Works* (hereafter EW), *The Middle Works* (MW), and *The Later Works* (LW). In the essays ahead, a reference to LW.5.270, for example, will mean *The Later Works*, Volume 5, page 270. [The pagination of the print edition has been preserved in *The Collected Works of John Dewey 1882-1953: The Electronic Edition*, edited by Larry A. Hickman and published by InteLex Corporation, Charlottesville, Virginia (1996).]

CHAPTER 6

1. In what follows regarding hermeneutics, I draw on the work of Hans-Georg Gadamer and Richard Rorty as well as on an account of their theories that I develop in Arcilla (1995).

2. To be sure, it must be acknowledged that this principle of reading has been under steady attack by deconstructionists and can no longer be adopted without argument. An adequate response to this critique, however, would take us far beyond the bounds of this essay's concerns. For now, then, I propose this protocol of reading in the hope that it will seem plausible enough to consider if hardly uncontroversial.

3. I am especially mindful of Jackson's roots in the alternative philosophical tradition of Dewey, which Robert Boostrom, and David Granger and Craig Cunningham, have documented in their essays in this volume (Chapters 5 and 11, respectively).

CHAPTER 11

1. Jackson suggests that Dewey looks to do something similar in his writing: "What Dewey does is to enact in the writing itself several of those very qualities upon which he is reporting—that things fit together organically rather than mechanically, for example, or that endings and beginnings are arbitrary designations rather than definitive ones. Those attributes then become for his readers part of the qualitative immediacy of the reading experience" (1998b, p.160).

2. The general conclusions recounted here may seem somewhat disconnected from the kinds of practical issues that confront schools and society today, such as accountability, funding disparities, local versus state and federal control, and so on. However, Jackson remains convinced that having a general sense of the role of the forms or practices of experience provides valuable perspective on such issues. He is currently looking closely at Dewey's many published essays on practical (even political) topics in search of further evidence for the value of the generalizations produced by an empirical metaphysics.

3. Around the same time, Jackson was also invited to address a conference of art educators. The resulting piece, which deals with the precarious place of the arts in today's schools, was entitled "Thinking About the Arts in Education: A Reformed Perspective," and later appeared in the *Teachers College Record* (Jackson, 1994). As with much of the general literature in arts education, however, there is no explicit discussion here of either Dewey or Dewey's aesthetics. Jackson (1995) later suggests that this shortfall in the literature was part of what prompted his subsequent foray into Dewey's aesthetics.

References

Arcilla, R. V. (1995). *For the love of perfection: Richard Rorty and liberal education*. New York: Routledge.

Auden, W. H. (1975). Under which lyre: A reactionary tract for the times, Phi Beta Kappa Poem, Harvard University, 1946. In Auden, *Collected Shorter Poems, 1927-1957* (pp. 221-226). New York: Vintage.

Banks, J. A. (1993). Multicultural education: Historical development, dimensions, and practice. In L. Darling-Hammond (Ed.), *Review of Research in Education* (Vol. 19) (pp. 3-50). Washington, DC: American Educational Research Association.

Boisvert, R. (1988). *Dewey's metaphysics*. New York: Fordham University Press.

Boostrom, R. E., Hansen, D.T., & Jackson, P. W. (1993). Coming together and staying apart: How a group of teachers and researchers sought to bridge the "research-practice gap." *Teachers College Record, 94*, 35-44.

Bush, G. W. (2005). Press conference. Retrieved July 6, 2006, from http://www.whitehouse.gov/news/releases/2005/10/20051004-1.html

Cavell, S. (1988). *In quest of the ordinary: Lines of skepticism and romanticism*. Chicago: University of Chicago Press.

Costantino, T. E. (2001). [*John Dewey and the Lessons of Art*]. Retrieved June 16, 2006, from http://edrev.asu.edu/reviews/rev135.htm

Costigan, A. T., & Crocco, M. S. (2004). *Learning to teach in an age of accountability*. Mahwah, NJ: Erlbaum.

Cremin, L. A. (1965). *The genius of American education*. Pittsburgh: University of Pittsburgh Press.

Darling-Hammond, L. (1996). *The right to learn*. San Francisco: Jossey-Bass.

Darling-Hammond, L. (1998). Experience and education: Implications for teaching and schooling today. In J. Dewey, *Experience and Education: The 60th anniversary edition*. West Lafayette, IN: Kappa Delta Pi.

Darling-Hammond, L., Banks, J., Zumwalt, K., et al. (2005). Educational goals and purposes: Developing a curricular vision for teaching. In L. Darling-Hammond & J. Bransford (Eds.), *Preparing teachers for a changing world: What teachers should learn and be able to do* (pp. 169-200). San Francisco: Jossey-Bass.

Darling-Hammond, L., French, J., & Garcia-Lopez, S. P. (2002). *Learning to teach for social justice*. New York: Teachers College Press.

Dewey, J. (1972). Plan of organization for the University Primary School. In *John Dewey, the early works 1882-1898: Vol. 5. Early essays* (J. A. Boydston, Ed.) (pp. 224-243). Carbondale: Southern Illinois University Press.

Dewey, J. (1981). *John Dewey, the later works 1925-1953: Vol. 1. Experience and nature* (J. A. Boydston, Ed.). Carbondale: Southern Illinois University Press.

Dewey, J. (1983). *John Dewey, the middle works 1899-1924: Vol. 14. Human nature and conduct 1922* (J. A. Boydston, Ed.). Carbondale: Southern Illinois University Press.

Dewey, J. (1985). *John Dewey, the middle works 1899-1924: Vol. 9. Democracy and education 1916* (J. A. Boydston, Ed.). Carbondale: Southern Illinois University Press.

Dewey, J. (1987). *John Dewey, the later works 1925-1953: Vol. 10. Art as experience* (J. A. Boydston, Ed.). Carbondale: Southern Illinois University Press.

Dewey, J. (1988). Experience and education. In *John Dewey, the later works 1925-1953: Vol. 13. Experience and education, Freedom and culture, Theory of valuation and essays* (J. A. Boydston, Ed.) (pp. 1-62). Carbondale: Southern Illinois University Press.

Dewey, J. (1989). How we think. In *John Dewey, the later works 1925-1953: Vol. 8. Essays and How we think, revised edition* (J. A. Boydston, Ed.) (pp. 105-352). Carbondale: Southern Illinois University Press.

Dickinson, E. (1960). The gleam of a heroic act. In *The Complete Poems of Emily Dickenson* (T. H. Johnson, Ed.) (pp. 688-689). Boston: Little Brown. (Original work published 1891)

Donoghue, D. (1986). *We Irish: Essays on Irish literature and society*. New York: Knopf.

Dunkin, M., & Biddle, B. (1974). *The study of teaching*. New York: Holt, Rinehart & Winston.

Eisner, E. W. (1995). *The hidden consequences of a national curriculum*. Washington, DC: American Educational Research Association.

Elkins, J. (1996). *The object stares back*. San Diego: Harcourt Brace & Company.

Freire, P. (1998). *Teachers as cultural workers: Letters to those who dare to teach*. Boulder, CO: Westview.

Frost, R. (1972). The Figure a poem makes: An introduction. In *Robert Frost: Poetry and prose* (E. C. Lathem & L. Thompson, Eds.) (pp. 393-396). New York: Holt Rinehart & Winston. (Original work published 1939)

Garrison, J. W. (1985). Dewey and the empirical unity of opposites. *Transactions of the Charles S. Peirce Society, 21*, 549-561.

Geertz, C. (1983). Blurred genres: The refiguration of social thought. In Geertz, *Local Knowledge* (pp. 19-35). New York: Basic Books.

Getzels, J. W., & Jackson, P. W. (1962). *Creativity and intelligence: Explorations with gifted students*. New York: Wiley.

Getzels, J. W., & Jackson, P. W. (1963). The teacher's personality and characteristics. In N. L. Gage (Ed.), *Handbook of Research on Teaching* (pp. 506-582). Chicago: Rand McNally.

Hansen, D. T. (1989). Getting down to business: The moral significance of classroom beginnings. *Anthropology and Education Quarterly, 20*, 259-274.

Hansen, D. T. (1995). *The call to teach*. New York: Teachers College Press.

Hansen, D. T. (1996). In class with Philip W. Jackson. In C. Kridel, R. V. Bullough, & P. Shaker (Eds.), *Mentoring: Portraits of and by distinguished 20th century educators* (pp. 127-138). Hamden, CT: Garland.

Hegel, G. W. F. (1991). *Elements of the philosophy of right*. Cambridge: Cambridge University Press. (Original work published 1821)

Heidegger, M. (1962). *Kant and the problem of metaphysics*. Bloomington: Indiana University Press. (Original work published 1929)

Heidegger, M. (1996). *Being and time* (J. Stambaugh, Trans.). Albany: State University of New York Press. (Original work published 1953)

Hesse, H. (1969). *The glass bead game (Magister Ludi)* (R. Winston & C. Winston, Trans.). New York: Holt, Rinehart & Winston. (Original work published 1943)

Hillesum, E. (1996). *An interrupted life* (A. J. Pomerans, Trans.). New York: Henry Holt. (Original work published 1981)

Holderlin, F. (1990). *Selected poems* (D. Constantine, Trans.). Newcastle-upon-Tyne, UK: Bloodaxe Books.

Jackson, P. W. (1968). *Life in classrooms*. Austin, TX: Holt, Rinehart & Winston.

Jackson, P. W. (1975). Shifting visions of the curriculum: Notes on the aging of Franklin Bobbitt. *The Elementary School Journal, 75*, 118-133.

Jackson, P. W. (1977). Lonely at the top: Observations on the genesis of administrative isolation. *School Review, 85*(3), 425-432.

Jackson, P. W. (1981a). Secondary schooling for children of the poor. *Daedalus, 110*(4), 39-57.

Jackson, P. W. (1981b). Comprehending a well-run comprehensive: A report on a visit to a large suburban high school. *Daedalus, 110*(4), 81-95.

Jackson, P. W. (1981c). Secondary schooling for the privileged few: A report on a visit to a New England boarding school. *Daedalus, 110*(4), 117-130.

Jackson, P. W. (1982). John Dewey's poetry. *American Journal of Education, 91*(1), 65-78.

Jackson, P. W. (1983). The reform of science education: A cautionary tale. *Daedalus, 112*(2), 143-166.

Jackson, P. W. (1986). *The practice of teaching*. New York: Teachers College Press.

Jackson, P. W. (1987, August–September). Mainstreaming art: An essay on discipline-based art education. *Educational Researcher*, pp. 39-43.

Jackson, P. W. (1990a). The functions of educational research. *Educational Researcher, 19*, 3-9.

Jackson, P. W. (1990b). Introduction. In P. W. Jackson, *Life in Classrooms* (reissue). New York: Teachers College Press.

Jackson, P.W. (1990c). Introduction. In J. Dewey, *The child and the curriculum* and *The school and society*. Chicago: University of Chicago Press.

Jackson, P. W. (1992a). The enactment of the moral in what teachers do. *Curriculum Inquiry, 22*, 401-407.

Jackson, P. W. (1992b). *Untaught lessons*. New York: Teachers College Press.

Jackson, P. W. (Ed.). (1992c). *Handbook of research on curriculum*. New York: Macmillan.

Jackson, P. W. (1994). Thinking about the arts in education: A reformed perspective. *Teachers College Record, 95*(4), 542-554.

Jackson, P. W. (1995). If we took Dewey's aesthetics seriously, how would art be taught? In J. Garrison (Ed.), *The new scholarship on Dewey* (pp. 25-34). Dordrecht, The Netherlands: Kluwer.

Jackson, P. W. (1998a). Dewey's *Experience and Education* revisited. In J. Dewey, *Experience and education: The 60th anniversary edition*. West Lafayette, IN: Kappa Delta Pi.

Jackson, P. W. (1998b). *John Dewey and the lessons of art*. New Haven, CT: Yale University Press.

Jackson, P. W. (2002a). Dewey's 1906 definition of art. *Teachers College Record, 104*(2), 167-177.

Jackson, P. W. (2002b). *John Dewey and the philosopher's task*. New York: Teachers College Press.

Jackson, P. W., Boostrom, R. E., & Hansen, D. T. (1993). *The moral life of schools*. San Francisco: Jossey-Bass.

James, T. (1990). Kurt Hahn and the aims of education. *Journal of Experiential Education, 13*, 6-13.

JPS Hebrew-English Tanakh: *The Traditional Hebrew Text and the New JPS*. Translation. (1999). Philadelphia: Jewish Publication Society.

Kliebard, H. M. (1979). Systematic curriculum development, 1890-1959. In J. Schaffarzick & G. Sykes (Eds.), *Values conflicts and curriculum issues* (pp. 197-236). Berkeley, CA: McCutchan.

Lewis, A. C. (2006). Washington commentary: Redefining what high school students learn. *Phi Delta Kappan, 87*(8), 564-565.

Lightfoot, S. L. (1983). *The good high school: Portraits of character and culture*. New York: Basic Books.

Lortie, D. C. (1975). *Schoolteacher: A sociological study*. Chicago: University of Chicago Press.

Martin, J. R. (1976). What should we do with a hidden curriculum when we find one? *Curriculum Inquiry, 6*(2), 135-151.

Melville, H. (1981). *Moby Dick*. Berkeley: University of California Press. (Original work published 1851)

Merleau-Ponty, M. (1964). Eye and mind. In J. M. Edie (Ed.), *The primacy of perception* (pp. 159-190). Evanston, IL: Northwestern University Press.

Montaigne, M. (1991). On educating children. In *Michel de Montaigne: The complete essays* (M. A. Screech, Trans.) (pp. 163-199). New York: Penguin. (Original work published 1592)

Murdoch, I. (1970). *The sovereignty of good*. London: Ark.

Nagel, T. (2004). Much ado. *Times Literary Supplement, 7*, 3.

National Commission on Excellence in Education. (1983). *A nation at risk*. Washington, D.C.: Author.

Phillips, D. C., & Burbules, N. C. (2000). *Postpositivism and educational research*. Lanham, MD: Rowman & Littlefield.

Rabinow, P., & Sullivan, W. M. (Eds.). (1979). *Interpretive social science: A reader.* Berkeley: University of California Press.

Rilke, R. M. (1989). The ninth Duino elegy. In *The selected poetry of Rainer Maria Rilke* (S. Mitchell, Trans.) (pp. 198–203). New York: Vintage International. (Original work published 1923)

Rundle, B. (2004). *Why there is something rather than nothing.* Oxford: Oxford University Press.

Schwab, J. J. (1969). The practical: A language for curriculum. *School Review, 78*(1), 1–23.

Sergiovanni, T. (1992). *Moral leadership.* San Francisco: Jossey Bass.

Shulman, L. (1983). Autonomy and obligation. In L. Shulman & G. Sykes (Eds.), *Handbook of teaching and policy* (pp. 484–504). White Plains, NY: Longman.

Sizer, T. (1984). *Horace's compromise: The dilemma of the American high school.* Boston: Houghton Mifflin.

Sleeper, R. W. (1986). *The necessity of pragmatism: John Dewey's conception of philosophy.* New Haven: Yale University Press.

Smith, L., & Geoffrey, W. (1968). *The complexities of an urban classroom: An analysis toward a general theory of teaching.* New York: Holt, Rinehart & Winston.

Snyder, J., Bolin, F., & Zumwalt, K. (1992). Curriculum implementation. In P. W. Jackson (Ed.), *Handbook of research on curriculum,* (pp. 402–435). New York: Macmillan.

Stark, J. (2006). Big names not likely to get traded, ESPN. Retrieved June 16, 2006, from http://sports.espn.go.com/mlb/columns/story?columnist=stark_jayson&id =2485721

Starnes, B. A. (2006). Thoughts on teaching: On nerds, science education, and horror films. *Phi Delta Kappan, 87*(8), 634–635.

Stevens, W. (1982a). The man with the blue guitar. In Stevens, *The collected poems of Wallace Stevens.* New York: Vintage. (Original work published 1937)

Stevens, W. (1982b). Notes toward a supreme fiction. In Stevens, *The collected poems of Wallace Stevens.* New York: Vintage. (Original work published 1942)

Stravinsky, I. (1970). *Poetics of music in the form of six lessons.* Cambridge, MA: Harvard University Press. (Original work published 1942)

Tanner, L. N. (1997). *Dewey's Laboratory School: Lessons for today.* New York: Teachers College Press.

Tyack, D. B. (1997). Ways of seeing: An essay on the history of compulsory schooling. In R. M. Jaeger (Ed.), *Complementary methods for research in education* (2nd ed.) (pp. 35–69). Washington, DC: American Educational Research Association.

Warnock, M. (1978). *Imagination.* Berkeley: University of California Press.

Winerip, M. (2006, July 12). Teachers, and a law that distrusts them. *The New York Time,* p. B8.

Wittgenstein, L. (1953). *Philosophical investigations* (G. E. M. Anscombe, Trans.). New York: Macmillan.

Wittgenstein, L. (1961). *Tractatus logico-philosophicus* (D. F. Pears & B. F. McGuinness, Trans.). Atlantic Highlands, NJ: Humanities Press. (Original work published 1921)

Yeats, W. B. (1956). *Collected poems*. New York: Macmillan.

Zumwalt, K. (1989). Beginning professional teachers: The need for a curricular vision of teaching. In M. C. Reynolds (Ed.), *Knowledge base for beginning teachers* (pp. 173–184). Oxford: Pergamon Press.

Zumwalt, K. (1995). What's a national curriculum anyway? In E. W. Eisner (Ed.), *The hidden consequences of a national curriculum* (pp. 1–12). Washington, DC: American Educational Research Association.

Zumwalt, K. (2004). Choosing to make a difference. In A. T. Costigan & M. S. Crocco (Eds.), *Learning to teach in an age of accountability* (pp. 247–257). Mahwah, NJ: Erlbaum.

About the Editors and the Contributors

René V. Arcilla (Editor) is currently Associate Professor of Educational Philosophy and Chair of the Department of Humanities and the Social Sciences in the Professions at New York University's Steinhardt School. He earned a Ph.D. in Education from the University of Chicago in 1990. He is the author of numerous articles and of *For the Love of Perfection: Richard Rorty and Liberal Education*. His scholarly and teaching interests include philosophy of education, liberal learning, existentialism, and modernism. Recently, he has been working on a theory of modernism as a culture of existential learning.

Robert Boostrom worked with Philip Jackson and David Hansen on the Moral Life of Schools project. Since then he has been with the Department of Teacher Education at the University of Southern Indiana. He is the author of *Thinking*.

Craig A. Cunningham is Associate Professor at National College of Education of National-Louis University in Chicago, where he directs the program in Technology in Education and also teaches courses in the history and philosophy of education. Cunningham is author, with Marty Billingsley, of *Curriculum Webs: Weaving the Web into Teaching and Learning*, as well as articles dealing with moral education, the history of American education, John Dewey's work, and the use of the Internet in education. He holds a Ph.D. in Philosophy of Curriculum from the University of Chicago, where Philip Jackson supervised his dissertation on *The Moral Consequences of John Dewey's Metaphysics*.

Linda Darling-Hammond is Charles E. Ducommun Professor of Education at Stanford University, where she has served as the faculty sponsor of the Stanford Teacher Education Program and co-founder of the Stanford Educational Leadership Institute. Her research, teaching, and policy work focus on teaching quality, school reform, and educational equity.

Mary Erina Driscoll (Editor) is Associate Professor of Educational Administration in the Steinhardt School of Education at New York University. She earned her Ph.D. in education from the University of Chicago in 1989. Her research focuses on the connections between schools and their communities and the ways in which school–community relationships provide a context for student learning. Currently, she is engaged in a national study of some of the schools and school districts that enrolled students displaced by Hurricane Katrina.

Elliot W. Eisner is Lee Jacks Professor Emeritus at Stanford University. His major interests are in arts education, curriculum studies, and qualitative research methodology. He has held many posts, including president of the American Education Research Association and president of the John Dewey Society.

David A. Granger received his Ph.D. in Philosophy of Education from the University of Chicago in 1998. He is now Associate Professor of Education at the State University of New York at Geneseo, where he currently serves as the coordinator of the Childhood Education Program. He is the author of *John Dewey, Robert Pirsig, and the Art of Living: Revisioning Aesthetic Education*, and has published numerous articles on John Dewey and aesthetic education in journals, including *Educational Theory*, *Studies in Philosophy and Education*, the *Journal of Aesthetic Education*, the *Journal of Curriculum Studies*, *Teachers College Record*, and *Educational Change*.

Maxine Greene holds a Ph.D. in Philosophy of Education from New York University and several honorary degrees. She is Professor Emerita of Philosophy and Education at Teachers College, Columbia University, and continues to teach in the program as an adjunct professor. She is also Philosopher in Residence at the Lincoln Center Institute for the Arts in Education. Her former positions include William F. Russell Professor in the Foundations of Education at Teachers College and presidencies of the American Educational Research Association, the Philosophy of Education Society, and the American Educational Studies Association. She has published six books, including *Teacher as Stranger*, *Releasing the Imagination*, and *The Dialectic of Freedom*.

David T. Hansen (Editor) is Professor and director of the program in Philosophy and Education at Teachers College, Columbia University, and is immediate past president of the John Dewey Society. He earned his B.A. and Ph.D. degrees from the University of Chicago. His scholarship focuses on the philosophy and practice of teaching, and he has been working on a project to reimagine the humanistic roots of education. He has recently published *John Dewey and Our Educational Prospect: A Critical Engagement with Dewey's* Democracy and Education.

Thomas James is dean and Professor of Educational History in the School of Education at the University of North Carolina at Chapel Hill. After earning his Ph.D. at Stanford University, he worked at Wesleyan, Brown, and New York Universities before arriving to UNC in 2004. His current interests include the history of education, public policy and school governance, and experiential education.

Lee S. Shulman is the eighth President of the Carnegie Foundation for the Advancement of Teaching. Prior to this, he was the first Charles E. Ducommun Professor of Education Emeritus at Stanford University. He is a past president of the American Educational Research Association and a Fellow of the American Academy of Arts & Sciences. In 2006, Shulman was awarded the Grawemeyer Prize in Education for his collected papers on teaching and teacher education, published as *The Wisdom of Practice*.

Lauren A. Sosniak was Associate Professor of Teacher Education at San Jose State University at the time of her death in January 2006. A widely known and respected curriculum scholar, she studied curriculum development and implementation in schools, including in specific subject areas such as mathematics and science. In recent years, she had returned to her early career interest in the development of talent in both the young and old, and was drawing upon new field-based research.

Karen Zumwalt is the Edward Evenden Professor of Education, Department of Curriculum and Teaching, Teachers College, Columbia University. She studied with Philip Jackson at the University of Chicago while working on her Ph.D., at the time when he was metamorphosing into a Curriculum and Philosophy professor and also serving as director of the Laboratory School. Later, when Jackson was vice president of division B (Curriculum Studies) of the American Educational Research Association, she served as his program chair. Along with Jon Snyder and Fran Schoonmaker Bolin, she wrote a chapter on "Curriculum Implementation" for the *Handbook on Curriculum Research* that Jackson edited.

Index